WHAT IS HISTORY TODAY . . . ?

Related Macmillan titles

E. H. Carr, *What is History?*
Arthur Marwick, *The Nature of History*
R. F. Atkinson, *Knowledge and Explanation in History*
Barbara W. Tuchman, *Practising History*

WHAT IS
HISTORY TODAY . . . ?

Edited by
Juliet Gardiner

MACMILLAN

First published 1988 by
THE MACMILLAN PRESS LTD
Houndmills, Basingstoke, Hampshire RG21 2XS
and London
Companies and representatives
throughout the world

ISBN 0–333–42225–2 hardcover
ISBN 0–333–42226–0 paperback

A catalogue record for this book is available
from the British Library.

Printed in Hong Kong

Reprinted 1989, 1990, 1992, 1993

The articles in this book (with the exception of those by Paul
Dukes and Douglas Johnson) were published in *History
Today* from December 1984 to January 1986. The editor and
publishers wish to thank History Today for permission to
reproduce them.

CONTENTS

Introduction   1

1. WHAT IS MILITARY HISTORY?   4
Michael Howard, Brian Bond, J. C. A. Stagg,
David Chandler, Geoffrey Best, John Terraine

2. WHAT IS POLITICAL HISTORY?   18
T. P. Wiseman, G. R. Elton, Ronald Hutton,
Roy Foster, John Turner, Kenneth O. Morgan

3. WHAT IS ECONOMIC HISTORY?   31
D. C. Coleman, Roderick Floud, T. C. Barker,
M. J. Daunton, N. F. R. Crafts

4. WHAT IS SOCIAL HISTORY?   42
Raphael Samuel, John Breuilly, J. C. D. Clark,
Keith Hopkins, David Cannadine

5. WHAT IS RELIGIOUS HISTORY?   58
Patrick Collinson, Christopher Brooke, Edward Norman,
Peter Lake, David Hempton

6. WHAT IS THE HISTORY OF SCIENCE?   69
Roy Porter, Steven Shapin, Simon Schaffer,
Robert M. Young, Roger Cooter, Maurice Crosland

7. WHAT IS WOMEN'S HISTORY?   82
Olwen Hufton, Natalie Zemon Davis, Sally Humphreys,
Angela V. John, Linda Gordon

8. WHAT IS THE HISTORY OF ART?   96
Alex Potts, John House, Charles Hope,
Tom Gretton

9. WHAT IS INTELLECTUAL HISTORY?   105
Stefan Collini, Quentin Skinner, David A. Hollinger,
J. G. A. Pocock, Michael Hunter

10. WHAT IS THE HISTORY OF POPULAR CULTURE?   120
   Asa Briggs, Peter Burke, Dai Smith,
     Jeffrey Richards, Stephen Yeo

11. WHAT IS DIPLOMATIC HISTORY?   131
   D. C. Watt, Simon Adams, Roger Bullen,
     Kinley Brauer, Akira Iriye

12. WHAT IS EUROPEAN HISTORY?   143
A. J. P. Taylor, Paul Dukes, Immanuel Wallerstein,
   Douglas Johnson, Marc Raeff, Eva Haraszti

13. WHAT IS THIRD WORLD HISTORY?   155
 M. E. Yapp, C. A. Bayly, Gervase Clarence Smith,
Christopher Abel, Gordon Johnson, Christopher Fyfe

INTRODUCTION

'What is History?' asked E. H. Carr nearly a quarter of a century ago, and one of the ways he explored this question was to define the pursuit of history as 'an unending dialogue between the present and the past'. It was in the belief that this unending dialogue has taken fundamentally new avenues since Professor Carr first asked his influential question that, in 1984–85, the magazine *HISTORY TODAY* decided to pose the question what is history? afresh, and in ways that it was hoped were in keeping with these new approaches.

Although in the 1980s, there can no longer be the same confidence in the inevitable expansion of reason, or the same belief in the growing self-awareness of historians in their interpretation of the past, as characterised Carr's work in the 1960s, what is evident is an increasingly ambitious approach to subject matter, about what is a proper area for historical enquiry, from constitutions to forgery, from magic to menstruation.

It is not only as a result of technical innovations that restricted conceptions of the substance of history have widened. The study of archaeology may have been transformed by the application of new techniques, but it hardly takes new technology to make women visible. This stretching of the historical canvas is largely as a result of the educational, social and political experience of those writing and reading history. It is in this spirit that the contours of the past have been remapped; existing questions have been reformulated; known 'facts' have been reinterrogated; what was once considered marginal has been woven into the centrality of historical enquiry and historical research has been recognised as a more profound exercise than simply 'filling in the gaps'.

How does this definition by concept and by approach rather than by chronology, this belief that it is illuminating to identify, for example, women's history, third world history, labour history, delineate the question, 'What is History?'

One answer might be that it fragments and atomises the past so that we are left with nothing but the loose change of history. It subdivides where no division is possible and it renders any expectation of a synthesis hopeless: the chances of a coherent narrative history, the possibility of putting the story of the past back together again, are lost forever. They are dispersed on a fashionable breeze of specialisation the logical conclusion of which would be that history ceased to have any status as a separate discipline at all and simply became a prefix attached to the various influences upon it: the history of politics, of sociology, of science or of economics, as a strand in the present.

1

But this demarcation is, in any case false, since whatever label an historian cares to stick on his or her subject, no demarcation can be total. If one looks, for example, at the case of tariff regulations: their imposition is strictly a political act, concerned with the assessment by politicians of the necessity for and popularity of such measures in political terms: equally, the effects and need for such regulations concern the economic historian, preoccupied as he or she must be with balance of payments, terms of trade, supply and demand; the social historian will be interested in the effects on workers, on labour mobility, on the depression of wages, or the reverse: and to subdivide further, there are rich pickings too for the labour historian, so-styled, the students of women's history, and no doubt for the historian of the third world.

The retreat from faith in impartial 'truth', the loss of the belief in the past as a jigsaw which will one day be complete, the desire to bring the past nearer to the boundaries of people's lives, have all animated a new pluralism which the historians in this book seek to discuss. The responses to the question 'What is history?' posed in these ways are very varied: there are those who find any attempt to dissect the corpus of the past under categorical labels untenable and unhelpful; others welcome the opportunity to explain how wide their own particular areas are – how religious history, perhaps, was concerned with man's place in society as much as with his formal belief system. Some historians emphasise the instrumentality of new insights; whilst others feel their own particular areas to have been consigned a label only in the vacuum seemingly left by the emergence of newer historical constructs.

The result is a series of manifestos, apologias, pleas, explorations, explanations and denials which bear eloquent testimony to the diversity of approach of historians writing today. It also rejoices in that diversity: it nurtures a scepticism that phrases like 'national spirit' or 'baroque mentality' be thought explicatory of anything at all: it gives the lie to the spurious hope of 'coherence'. In the words of Theodore K. Rabb 'there can no longer be a plausible expectation that an omnicompetent polymath or paradigm setter will unite us all'.

Nothing will have been lost and all will have been gained if this enthusiasm for divergence and for the particular enables the historian to fulfil John Donne's belief that history 'makes a little room an everywhere'.

2

It goes without saying that without the historians – unfortunately more than it was possible to represent here – who were prepared to examine their art and define their craft, this book would not have been possible. Nor would it have been possible without the practical enthusiasm of my colleagues at *HISTORY TODAY*, Jacqueline Guy, Celia Jones, Marion Soldan, Doris Lynch and Sarah Guy. It was Vanessa Couchman at Macmillan who decided that these questions were worth asking – and answering – between hard covers.

Juliet Gardiner
November 1986

1. WHAT IS
MILITARY HISTORY . . . ?

*The story of campaigns and battles? The assessment of
leaders, tactics and strategy? The retirement task of old
soldiers? A luxury enjoyed by peaceful societies? History's
most passionate dramas? The mainstay of western
historiography? Narrow technicalities? An inseparable part
of the study of society? What is military history?*

Michael Howard

'Military history' can be simply defined as the history of armed
forces and the conduct of war, and for many years it was a discrete,
finite, specialist study. In the United Kingdom it emerged during
the eighteenth century, with studies of Marlborough's wars on the
continent and of what were generically described as 'the wars in
Germany'. It developed with studies of the Napoleonic wars,
especially the Peninsular and Waterloo campaigns, and the campaigns of the British armies in North America and India. By the mid-
nineteenth century the prime characteristics of British military
historiography were clear.

'Military history' was the study of the campaigns of a small,
volunteer British army, fighting, invariably overseas, against either
a comparable European force or inchoate 'native' armies. So far as
British society as a whole was concerned, they might have been
fighting on the moon.

During the great expansion of British historical studies in the
latter half of the nineteenth century, military history remained a
subject apart, a small backwater attracting only members of the
armed services and their fellow travellers. Naval history was in little
better shape. The connection between naval success and national
survival was clear to all historians of the Elizabethan age from
Froude onward, while that between sea power and imperial
expansion had been pointed out by English writers like the Colomb
brothers even before Mahan published his deceptively simple
theories in the 1890s. But any serious analysis of the relationship
between British naval and economic strength had to await Paul
Kennedy's *The Rise and Fall of British Naval Mastery*, published in
1976.

Military history was thus in Britain a 'special subject' with which few serious scholars concerned themselves. Even the attempts by patriotic universities to revive it before 1914 had very limited success. Colonel G. F. R. Henderson saw that the American Civil War had significantly different lessons to teach from the European campaigns, but even his studies became the narrowest of campaign histories which stressed the similarities with the Napoleonic wars rather than the differences. For nearly half a century the Chair of Military History at Oxford was occupied by journalists or retired soldiers, who made little effort to broaden the scope of their subject. Yet even before 1914 the traditional concept of military history was archaic, as continental historians were very well aware.

For the British, the Revolutionary and Napoleonic Wars were qualitatively little different from those which preceded them: invasion threats thwarted by naval supremacy, small colonial campaigns, continental intervention by a small regular force whose contribution to the final victory was understandably exaggerated. To the continental powers, however, those wars brought military, political and social transformation. Clausewitz was not unique in perceiving that after them things could never be the same again; but he saw more clearly than most that the limited warfare of the eighteenth century was not the norm it was assumed to be by British historians, but the product of a particular social and political structure that had had its day. War had now to be studied, as Hans Delbrück was to study it, in the framework of social and political history. It was clear to continental historians between 1870 and 1914, like Bernhardi and von der Goltz, that social and political as well as technological change would transform for better or worse, the nature of war. Even so, the only change they could conceive was one of scale: the wars of nations would in future be fought in larger and bloodier campaigns, but within the framework laid down by Napoleon and Moltke. Campaign history thus remained central to their interests, and what happened, or was likely to, away from the battlefield was left out of account.

The two World Wars changed all that. It might still be on the battlefield that decisions were reached, but the nature of the decision was so clearly determined by a multiplicity of factors – economic, technological, logistical, social, moral – that the history of those wars could not possibly be told purely in terms of their campaigns. The military historian might still focus on his traditional operational interests, but to understand and explain what happened during those operations he had to extend his interests so broadly as to make virtually a takeover bid for the writing of global history. Conversely, social and political historians of the belligerent countries, however disinclined they might be to soil their hands with so disreputable a subject as military history, had to acquire a working knowledge of it if they were to understand the impact of those wars on the societies they were studying.

In this respect historians were doing no more than returning to an older tradition. There is no 'military history' as such of classical antiquity, or even of the Middle Ages. These were societies organised for war, constantly at war, and their structure and their activity cannot be dissociated. 'Military history' as a speciality is a luxury which can be enjoyed only by atypically peaceful societies, and it is perhaps an indication of how peaceful our own society is today that military history in its narrowest operational sense should be enjoying so remarkable a boom. But underlying and behind all this lies the sombre need to study the history of war: to understand why our society is what it is, as well as what it might become.

Brian Bond

Clausewitz wrote that 'the decision by arms is for all major and minor operations in war what cash payment is in commerce'. By analogy all military history, though sometimes dealing with non-operational matters, must ultimately be related to war and combat. When I first began to specialise in military history, some twenty-five years ago, it was a badly neglected field among academics, partly no doubt because there were few established university posts in the subject. Regrettably this is still the case, though there has been a tremendous expansion in research and publications – as illustrated for example in the annual survey *War and Society Newsletter*, or in the London University list of theses in progress.

Twenty-five years ago there was also a sharper distinction between those who considered themselves to be military historians (nearly all former officers such as 'Boney' Fuller and Cyril Falls), and other historians with some interest in war. Traditional military history was essentially concerned with tactics and strategy; it tended to stress the significance of 'great captains' more than such aspects as war production, manpower allocation and civilian morale.

Sir Basil Liddell Hart, who died in 1970, was an outstanding practitioner in the traditional style whose qualities and limitations are evident in his last book, a *History of the Second World War*.

Although this kind of military history is still extremely popular (witness the outpouring of books on particular campaigns or battles of the two World Wars) many students of warfare are now concerned to place operations in their full historical context of war aims, the economic and social structure of warring states and the interaction between war and civil society. The Fontana *War and Society in Europe* series edited by Geoffrey Best, to which my own latest book was a contribution, epitomises the contemporary concern of military historians to portray war 'in the round'. Probably the outstanding individual influence on this trend has been that of Professor Michael Howard, whose teaching and publications both inculcate the importance of treating warfare in the broadest possible historical context. John Keegan was also surely right (in *The Face of Battle*) to argue that a great deal of traditional military history was stereotyped in its approach to combat and cliché-ridden in its descriptions: military historians in short can profit from the techniques and insights of allied disciplines. A good example, in my opinion, is Tony Ashworth's *Trench Warfare 1914–1918* (1980) which employs the sociologist's approach to examine the 'live and let live system' on the Western Front. Dr Ashworth's study also exemplifies a praiseworthy modern concern to pay due attention to the combat experience of ordinary fighting men as distinct from the staff and the high command. As long ago as 1969 Marc Ferro, co-director of the French journal *Annales*, broke away from the traditional campaign structure in his study *The Great War 1914– 1918*. More recently, following his trilogy on French military history from 1870 via Verdun to 1940 which brilliantly interwove the political and cultural strands, Alistair Horne has written a superb account of the Algerian conflict aptly entitled *A Savage War of Peace* (1977). This type of complex guerrilla war without clear-cut fronts and battles will surely provide the toughest challenge to military historians of the second half of the twentieth century.

Perhaps there is a tendency now to focus on 'the context' at the expense of the heart of the matter: war and combat. This is partly because many students are interested in such aspects as defence economics, weapons procurement and civil-military relations rather than war *per se*. Partly too in the nuclear age the notion has rightly gained acceptance that armed forces in most European countries exist primarily to deter rather than to wage war. The sudden and unexpected Falklands campaign was a salutary reminder that even in pacifistic democracies armed forces must, in the last resort, be able to fight.

Many laymen seem to identify the subject of military history, with the collection of militaria, or a fascination with regimental records and the minutiae of distant battles. These interests are perfectly respectable but they do not engage my interest compared to, say, large issues of military policy in peace-time and high level decision-making in war. At the other end of the spectrum to military antiquarianism, a great deal of writing about post-1945 defence issues lacks the essential historical ingredients of reasonably complete documentation and adequate perspective. It may be perfectly satisfactory as international relations or political science but not as history.

Although insufficiently appreciated in academic circles, I believe that military history, broadly interpreted as above, is quite as intrinsically important and as demanding a speciality as other branches of history. Its documentary sources, vast historiography and peculiar problems cannot easily be mastered in fleeting forays from other fields. 'War', Clemenceau asserted, was 'much too serious a thing to be left to the military'. Military history, however, *should* be left to the military historians – provided they take a broad and sophisticated view of their subject.

J. C. A. Stagg

Military history has long been one of the mainstays of western historiography. From the ancient Greeks through to the end of the nineteenth century the study of war – its causes, conduct, and consequences – has been a principal preoccupation of historians, and this concentration of historical effort was assumed to be a fair reflection of the importance of war in human affairs. Yet during the twentieth century, at a time when the significance of war for the human condition has never seemed to be greater, military history has fallen into relative disfavour and neglect, at least among serious historians. The reasons for this development are complex, but basically they centre on differing conceptions of history and its uses by the military and the historical professions. Consequently, military history today is a subject struggling towards a new sense of definition, one which must strive to restore it to something of its former primacy among the fields of historical endeavour.

Traditionally, much military history has been conventional in form, consisting of descriptive narratives about leading figures, campaigns, and decisive battles, while also providing assessments of the adequacy of generalship, strategy, and tactics. The focal point of these writings was often the battle, though, as John Keegan has noted, traditional military history seldom mastered the problems of explaining what actually occurred during these episodes of extreme violence. The chronological range of traditional military history, too, could be considerable, sometimes stretching from the ancient world to the Napoleonic era, and its practitioners often treated war as an abstract phenomenon from which predictable and logical themes, if not actual rules and laws, might be extracted. More varied was the degree to which historians related their discussions of the course of war to other factors – such as geography, climate, politics, administrative capacities, technology, and social and economic structures – that might have affected the performance of combatants. Here the political context of war-making was usually the most frequently studied factor, largely because war, in essence, has evolved into a form of conflict between nations and states.

Since the Second World War, however, the predominantly political approach to the study of history has given away to a broader range of social, economic, and cultural perspectives. This development has inevitably affected the practice of military history, though the full degree of its potential influence has yet to be felt. Nonetheless, much recent military history now proceeds from an awareness that wars are fought by large numbers of men (and sometimes women) whose needs and concerns can place unprecedented demands on the structures of society and the state. The way in which a nation wages war can be illuminated and transformed by an understanding of those whom a nation chooses to do its fighting, of how it chooses them, and of what happens to the people who experience military service and war. This interest in the social dimension of war has been reinforced by the realisation that the records of many military bureaucracies contain a great mass of very detailed information about large numbers of people who would otherwise remain obscure to professional historians. One striking example of how such records can be exploited is Fred Anderson's study of the social origins of Massachusetts' soldiers during the Seven Years' War which reveals that the conflict was much more of a 'people's war' than had been realised. Moreover, the strains of military mobilisation on Massachusetts society were very great, and that fact has now significantly influenced historians' understanding of the coming of the American Revolution and the war that occurred as its consequence.

Yet, in the last analysis, a truly satisfactory military history should consist of more than the narration and explanation of episodic violence, no matter how sophisticated this may be, and those episodes, in turn, should not be studied simply as reflections of larger patterns and problems in a society, no matter how rich these are in illustrative detail. Military history must redefine itself in the broadest sense as the study of societies at war, and its practitioners, ideally, should strive to understand war both as an instrument of state policy and as a process which can involve large numbers of people in violent experiences of considerable intensity. These experiences can often transform the people and the societies that undergo them. The recent writings of Richard Buel, Charles Royster, and John Shy on the nature and consequences of war in late eighteenth-century America are provocative examples of the potential for military history treated as the study of societies at war. Thus defined, military history can do justice to the various interests of all its practitioners, and in this form the subject may regain something of the pre-eminent status it once enjoyed among all historians.

David Chandler

To ask a military historian such a question is rather like asking Pontius Pilate to define 'truth'. In fact the enquiry involves two linked questions: not only 'What is military history?', but also 'What is it *for*?'. Of course there is no simple answer to either query, for there are many different shades of opinion as is perfectly right and proper if a subject is to remain dynamic. It must grow and develop and even explore what may turn out to be the occasional blind-alley. Each military historian must eventually reach his own position – without, it should be hoped, feeling impelled to denounce all that has gone before as irredentist nonsense or at best largely irrelevant *incunabula*.

'History', according to Dionysius of Halicarnassus, 'is experience teaching through examples'. Military history – as part of the broad spectrum of historical study – is in the simplest terms the study of 'Man in War'. It connotes a broad range of subjects inextricably linked to the military affairs of the past, including the human, social, institutional, political and technological aspects as well as the specifically professional sides of 'the bless'd trade'. Knowledge of the wars of the past can assist the understanding of the problems of the present, and even (with the hopes of avoiding the mistakes and misunderstandings that so tragically often give rise to recourse to armed struggles) help us to make some educated guesses about what the future may hold. Man's combative instincts have dominated most periods of the past, and even in the supposedly peaceful years since 1945 there have been over 200 identifiable wars fought at various levels affecting many countries in the Second and Third Worlds in particular. Indeed, the first recorded histories, by such famous names as Homer and Thucidydes, were largely devoted to accounts of human struggle, man against man, people against people. There has been little change.

Writing as a lecturer who, for approaching a quarter of a century, has been responsible for sharing in the education of successive generations of officer-cadets and young officers at Sandhurst, it has long been clear that military history itself (as understood in the professional sense) is only one part of the study of the kaleidoscope of warfare. The various strata lead on one from another to develop a comprehensive awareness of the complexities of the whole subject.

Thus military history (in the narrower sense of the study of campaigns, battles and leaders) is one foundation for war studies – the examination of the problems arising from the preparation for, and conduct of, war in the present century, particularly since 1945, together with the factors that have influenced those problems. Higher still up the scale come strategic studies – often the province of Staff Colleges – which have been described as:

> the study of modern military organisation, weapons and operations, and also the study of contemporary international and internal armed conflicts in their political, economic and military aspects; the role of alliances and other security systems; disarmament and arms control; strategic doctrines and national defence priorities.

Finally, at the level of the Royal Defence College, comes the consideration of grand strategy and national interest, of alliance policy, and the effective use of deterrence. Yet none of these several levels is mutually exclusive – but rather each draws as necessary from all that has preceded and indeed developed from it. We may hope that the senior planners of the South Atlantic Campaign of 1982 – once the political decision to act had been clearly communicated – took into account (or were at least aware of) the salient points that could be culled from the experiences of Suez, Normandy, Sicily, Gallipoli and even the Crimea (unopposed though the landing was, it was certainly on hostile soil) and Egypt (1801). Major-General Sir Jeremy Moore has mentioned that he found his knowledge of James Wolfe and Québec helpful in overcoming what Wavell called 'the loneliness of high command'. Thus military history has a part to play at all levels of a soldier's development – but above all at the foundation of his career when it is important to inculcate *esprit d'armée* in the aspiring officer. As Napoleon remarked, 'One must speak to the soul: it is the only way to electrify the man'.

I am also a military historian by inclination and interest in the fullest senses. Since sixth-form days at Marlborough, I have been fascinated by the military affairs of the past in general – and of the Marlburian and Napoleonic periods in particular. My particular focus is on the development of the military science and art, but I am also interested by the interplay of personality – the vital human element without which much else is, to me, somewhat meaningless. I am not a Tolstoian in that I am convinced that Napoleon made a lasting mark on the military aspects of his times – and on subsequent generations. For me, the subject does not at any level connote militarism any more than the study of medicine propagates disease. I do not hold with the view that a prime function of a military historian is to debunk legends and uncover misrepresentations.

Certainly he must report his findings if they do run counter to accepted belief, but the subject deserves more than this, and there are still large areas even in the Napoleonic area which are virtually *terra incognita*, and even more in the late seventeenth and early eighteenth centuries.

It is also much in my mind that the study of military history is not solely for the academic élite – its study is also an ideal source of pleasure for the layman with a genuine interest in the 'passionate dramas' of the past. Indeed, military history can be all things to all men. Almost any approach, providing it observes scholarly rules concerning the testing of evidence and the drawing of sustainable conclusions, is welcome – and all have a valuable role to play providing they accord the same toleration to other views that they require themselves. Even the disagreements – reflecting the greatest attributes of the subject in its many forms – are intellectually stimulating. As Professor Geyl remarked, 'History is an argument without end'.

Geoffrey Best

What do we go to the military historian for? Clearly not for the general history of war or for war's place in the general history of our species. Those big ventures in the war history business call on many expertises besides any merely military one. What the military historian can contribute to our understanding of history in general may be indispensible (besides whatever value it may have independently in its own right) but so will other sorts of historians' contributions be indispensible; economic, diplomatic, political and so on.

What then distinguishes the military history sort? I have long had a personal interest in this question. Did involvement in 'war and society' studies or research into the ethics and law of war make one a 'military historian'? By now I feel sure it didn't and doesn't. Military history's speciality, I conclude, is Battles and how to fight them, Campaigns and how to conduct them, and the ways armed forces gear themselves up for these special tasks. All the rest of the war-related work that has been going on since the 1960s under such descriptions as 'war studies' (Michael Howard, its founding father and continuing father-figure), 'war and society' (launched above all by Arthur Marwick and his team at the Open University) and 'armed forces and society' (Morris Janowitz's empire, strongly social-scientific) is, in its better bits and in its educational effects, magnificent – but it is not military history proper, and even the best of it may not include any proper military history at all.

The truth is that most of us dedicated to the study of armed forces and society whether in war or peace do not necessarily know much about the sharp end of our subject. This is nothing to be ashamed of. We may not need to know anything about it. The armed forces we hold steady in our sights exist and inter-relate with society and state whether they're at war or not; and most of them, for most of the time, are not. But their *raison d'être* nevertheless remains Fighting: for a minority of them, the fighting itself, and for the rest ('the tail'), support and supply of the fighters. Knowledge of how fighting is done, and what specifically military things and thoughts make it possible, is the military man's peculiar province, which outsiders can no more expect to enter without hard and humble study than they can expect to become proficient in theology, or solid geometry, or socio-linguistics.

Military history proper is a lot more complicated and technical than at first sight appears to historians like myself who are perhaps better described as 'militarily engaged'. Not presuming to speak for anyone other than myself, but rejoicing to have found myself one of very many non-military men and women enlarging and enriching the field of war studies by our involvement, an explanation of my limitations on the military history side, strictly defined, might run thus. First, so much of what was written by the military men who obviously were in a position to know what it took to manage armed forces and conduct battles was petty, parochial, and patriotic in the bad, anti-scientific way: narrow, complacent, insular. Put off by so much that was useless for serious scholarship other than the study of the mentality of those who wrote such stuff and those who read it, one missed the pearls of undoubted price lying in among the garbage. Second, the actual fighting in a war, about which military historians become most excited, did not seem to merit more weight in the total analysis of war than the many other elements (economic, psychological, cultural and so on) which military historians proper usually neglected and which demanded a bit of positive discrimination. Justifiably desirous of putting into the history of wars and warfare so much that warriors left out, one was prone to skip or skirt what they alone were sure to put in. War may indeed be too important to be left to the generals, but, after all, you can't wage it without any generals at all.

Military history, then, I judge to be the history of fighting and of the proximate means of fighting: military organisation and mentality, movement and logistics, weapons and equipment, strategic planning, tactical training, and battle behaviour. This is by no means the same as whole war history or the comprehensive understanding of the relations between armed forces and society upon which war history rests. But it is an inseparable part of it, and really good histories of wars and war-making include it. The first such a one which gave me a shock of recognition still seems to me a model of its kind: Michael Howard's *Franco-Prussian War*. But to describe that simply as 'military history' would be like calling Marilyn Monroe simply an 'actress'.

John Terraine

To date, the main thrust of my historical writing has been the military history of the First World War. I began in 1960 with a campaign narrative: *Mons: The Retreat to Victory*; nine more books about that war followed, the last of which, in 1982, *White Heat: The New Warfare 1914–19*, is unashamedly a study of its technology. I said in my Foreword:

> On the pages that follow there is very little strategy, scarcely any politics, no ideology and – I confess – almost no psychology. This is a book about the greatest First Industrial Revolution, war. In other words, it is about the very inner nature of the war, and may thus, I hope, illuminate its other aspects too.

I think this declares my hand: obviously, I must be a 'military historian', but more and more, in seeking to interpret the often amazing phenomena of the First World War, I saw it as the watershed of an industrial age. Before then, the technological revolution based on coal as a power source and steel as a material had been more or less controllable; afterwards, never. By this interpretation, it is evidently impossible to separate the military aspects from the productive forces of the societies that waged the war, or from the societies themselves. Modern military history, in other words, is not distinct from social history; it is a part of it – a very important part.

Three 'great' wars, with illuminating similarities, fall within the period during which the industrial states were based entirely or chiefly on the coal/steel technology: the American Civil War and the two World Wars. All, in expanding degrees, shared three fundamental features:

1 all three were fought *à outrance*, demanding the 'unconditional surrender', the absolute defeat, of one side or the other;
2 all three were wars of masses: armies of millions, huge fleets, finally vast air forces;
3 all three were immensely destructive of human life and all its appurtenances.

These three statements encapsulate the great wars of the epoch.

14

They are closely linked to each other: the 'total' war aim is intimately connected with the total involvement of large populations; the scale of death and destruction is intimately linked to the state of technology and the scale of mobilisation.

It is the capacity conferred by industrialisation that unifies the period, in war as in peace. The steam locomotive and the steamship, besides their economic significance, were also important social factors, conquering distance between communities and nations – and they were powerful instruments of war. The same, of course, is true of the international combustion engine in all its aspects; the agricultural tractor and the tank are blood-brothers; the conquest of the air was very soon seen as a means of conquering ground. Mass production clothed, equipped and fed the mass armies; even the homely sewing machine has its military history. Canned food transformed the problems of quartermasters as well as grocers. By 1917 a staff officer noted that at British GHQ:

> Nearly every one of the ramifications of civil law and life has its counterpart in the administrative departments . . . and for a population bigger than any single unit of control (except London) in England.

It is impossible to exaggerate this revolution in the military function.

In the First World War, a second industrial revolution, based on petroleum as a power source and increasingly using light metals, already played a large part, and an even larger in the Second, without ever displacing coal and steel. Electronics, a war instrument in America between 1861–65, made great advances between 1914–18, and still more between 1939–45. And in that war a Third Industrial Revolution, using plastics and computers, came to the fore with its new power source: atomic energy. So military history, in the modern world, displays a unity and continuum under the surface of constant change which derides all attempts to isolate its ingredients. It cannot be separated from the large, increasingly urban, populations, from their means of production and their productivity, from their technology and the techniques which it imposed. Nor can it be separated from their social systems, their physical condition and their ideologies. Armies, in the age of masses, are peoples in arms, putting their survival to the most critical test.

FURTHER READING

Aron, Jean-Paul *et al*, *Anthropologie du Conscrit Français d'après les Comptes Numériques et Sommaires du Recrutement de l'Armée (1819–26)*

(Paris, 1970); Anderson, F., *A People's Army: Massachusetts' Soldiers and Society in the Seven Year's War* (Chapel Hill, 1984); Atkinson, C. T., *Marlborough and the Rise of the British Army* (London, 1921); Baynes, J., *Morale* (London, 1967); Best, G., *Humanity in Warfare* (London, 1980); Bond, B., *Liddell Hart: A Study of his Military Thought* (London, 1977); *War and Society in Europe, 1870–1970* (London, 1977); Buel, R., Jnr, *Dear Liberty: Conneticut's Mobilization for the Revolutionary War* (Middletown, Conn., 1982); Butterfield, H., *Man's Attitude to the Past* (London, 1961); *Writings on Christianity and History* (Oxford, 1979); Clausewitz, *On War* (ed. Rapoport, A., trans. Graham, J. J., Harmondsworth, 1982); Fuller, General J. F. C., *The Decisive Battles of the Western World and their Influence on History* (three vols, London, 1954–56); Howard, M., 'The Uses and Abuses of Military History' in *The Causes of War* (London, 1983); *The Franco-Prussian War* (London, 1981); *Studies in War and Peace* (London, 1970); Keegan, J., *The Face of Battle* (London, 1976); Paret, P. (ed.), *Makers of Modern Strategy* (Princeton, 1986); Robertson, Field-Marshal Sir William, *Soldiers and Statesmen, 1914–1918* (two vols, London, 1926); Royster, C., *A Revolutionary People at War: The Continental Army and American Character, 1775–1783* (Chapel Hill, 1979); Shy, J., *A People Numerous and Armed: Reflections on the Military Struggle for Independence* (New York, 1976); Slim, Field-Marshal Sir William, *Defeat into Victory* (London, 1956); Spears, Major-General Sir Edward, *Liaison, 1914* (London, 1930); Strachen, H., *European Armies and the Conduct of War* (London, 1983); Tolstoy, L., *War and Peace* (trans. Carnett, C., London, 1971).

THE CONTRIBUTORS

Geoffrey Best's most recent bok is *War and Society in Revolutionary Europe* (London, 1982).

Brian Bond is Reader in War Studies at King's College, University of London, and author of *Liddell Hart: A Study of His Military Thought* (London, 1977).

David Chandler is Head of the Department of War Studies and International Affairs at the Royal Military Academy, Sandhurst, and author of *The Campaigns of Napoleon* (London, 1966) and *Napoleon's Marshals* (London, 1987).

Michael Howard is Regius Professor of Modern History at Oxford

University and Fellow of Oriel College. His most recent book is *Clausewitz* (Oxford, 1983).

J. C. A. Stagg is Senior Lecturer in American History at the University of Auckland and author of *Mr Madison's War: Politics, Diplomacy and Warfare in the Early American Republic, 1783–1830* (Princeton, 1983).

John Terraine's most recent book is *The Royal Airforce in the European War, 1939–45* (London, 1985).

2. WHAT IS
POLITICAL HISTORY . . . ?

*The introverted activities of a small élite of governors? The
record of institutional development? Narrow administrative
history? The most protean of the varieties of history? The
study of the organisation and operation of power in past
societies? What is political history?*

T. P. Wiseman

Political history is the history of the *polis*, the *res publica*, the citizen
body; political events are what was done by it, to it, or in its name.
Since a citizen body is made up of individuals, the rules which
constitute it are the basis of the subject. The first questions should
be: who? how? where? when? We need to know the limits of the
franchise, the machinery of citizen assembly, the frequency, physical conditions and rules of order of their meetings, the limits of their
decision-making powers. The citizen body usually deputes responsibility to a deliberative or advisory council: how were its members
chosen? how long did they serve? where, when and how were *their*
meetings held? It must choose executive officers to carry out its
decisions and look after the administration of its business: eligibil-
ity? means of election? length of service? extent of powers?

However obvious these practical questions are, it is essential to
start with them, to avoid anachronism and basic misunderstanding;
and it is better to carry on with them too, so that when it comes to
dealing with the enticing abstractions of policy and ideology, their
smeary colours may not wholly obscure a clear picture of real people
doing real things.

In every polity there are citizens for whom the strain, expense and
danger of political activism are outweighed by public spirit, family
tradition, desire for wealth or status, or an urge to get things (and
other people) sorted out – what we loosely call the pursuit of power.
The historian concentrates on these political leaders, and wants to
know the *modus operandi* – how each man gets himself elected, how
he gets his way in the council or assembly, what advantages he has
over his rivals, whether a persuasive tongue or a charismatic
presence outweighs wealth, patronage or a devoted retinue.

The dangers of ignoring practical questions are graphically
illustrated by the political interpreters of the Roman Republic. In the
nineteenth century, historians saw a two-party system of nobles

and *populares*; in the twentieth, they have seen 'factions' based on aristocratic families and their allies. Both models presuppose cooperation in pursuit of common ends as the norm in a polity where political life, and the traditional ethos of the political leaders, depended on competition and rivalry. Of course there were sometimes alliances, but they were temporary and *ad hoc*; of course there were sometimes great issues which divided the political élite, but never into 'parties' in any sense even approximately analogous to what modern English means by the term.

Instead of analysing the lists of yearly consuls into groups and factions to be endowed with a life of their own, it makes more sense to look hard at what first-hand evidence survives. In effect, that means Cicero, and particularly his correspondence. (There is no substitute for the authentic experience of a man in the thick of it, and Roman historians must face the unwelcome fact that the further away they get from Cicero's world, the more schematic and artificial their political history is bound to be.) Part of what Cicero shows us is perfectly familiar and intelligible in our own political terms – the country-house parties for advice on strategy, the counting of votes after a division in the Senate, the chanting crowds in the streets of the capital. But what we should concentrate on is the alien and unfamiliar – arson and torture, and senators spitting, weeping, grovelling on the ground and generally conducting themselves in public in a way quite inconsistent with our preconceived notion of Roman *gravitas*. That sort of scene is a healthy medicine against anachronism.

After 'who?', 'where?' and 'how?' comes the most seductive question: 'why?' Cicero's letters reveal a predictable juxtaposition of public and personal motives as he reports to Atticus on 'the state of the Republic' and 'my own position'. We have no such insight into the feelings of the ordinary citizen, but legislation on land distribution, debt relief and subsidised food gives us a fair indication of where his anxieties lay. Political issues and political motivation are where the danger of anachronism is greatest – not now because of the difference but because of the similarities. As Thucydides knew, while human nature remains the same the strong will do what they can and the weak will suffer what they must. But history is to do with particular cases, and the Roman experience should be interpreted on its own terms. It is breaking faith with the dead to use their political preoccupations as a way of attacking our own.

G. R. Elton

The present reaction against political history, though often ill-informed and sometimes silly, has its virtues. These arise less from the benefits conferred upon other ways of looking at the past than from the stimulus given to political history to improve itself. At heart, its function remains what it has always been: to study the manner in which groups of human beings have, through the ages, managed to organise their joint lives and conduct those affairs that determine relations within the group and with other groups outside it. Political history studies the history of man (and woman) in public action. It does not, however, confine itself to describing that action: it wishes to understand it. Thus it involves the analysis of law, constitution and administration, as well as (usually at second hand) a grasp of social and economic phenomena; it involves a good sense of minds and thoughts and attitudes; it demands an instructed analysis of the sources of action in the means of power and the demands of interests.

This may make the study of politics sound like a portmanteau affair, a vacuum cleaner sucking in the products of other forms of historical study. And so indeed in part it is and should be. Its low reputation stems from a time when it seemed to concern itself solely with the activities, often seen in a kind of social and intellectual vacuum, of kings and ministers, popes and bishops, foreign office clerks and members of parliament. Not only are those days long gone, but it is in fact quite difficult to find even past practitioners of such very arid historiography outside the ranks of writers of school textbooks and popular biographies whose activities no doubt helped to shape the hostile feelings of present critics in their formative years. This has been unfortunate. Leaving aside the fact that political history will always be pleasanter to read for a non-professional audience than the often highly technical studies that seek to supplant it, it should be said that political history enjoys two particular advances which render it essential for the healthy state of historical studies.

In the first place, it deals in people, even individuals, and not in statistical abstractions or notional groups (such as classes). The fashionable preference for social history always faces the danger of becoming merely anecdotal when it looks at 'real' people, and this, plus the illusion of accuracy offered by quantification, tends to drive such historians away from individuals. (Perhaps they don't actually much like them.) Political history inescapably places people at the centre of the enquiry, and the framework provided by the structure of government and the relationships of political beings with one another minimises the danger of anecdotalism. Only political history seems, for instance, capable of dealing effectively with war, one of mankind's commonest experiences which yet hardly ever puts in an appearance in other forms of history. The political historian's concerns drive him towards realities – towards what actually happened. They drive him away from dealing in abstract structures and forces which have reality only in the mind of the enquirer – if there.

Secondly, and most importantly, no other way of looking at history remains so continuously aware of the passage of time and the fact of change. Economic history can handle change, but its movement through time is very slow so that it tends to lose the sense of the hours passing. Social history of the advanced kind, strongly influenced by the social sciences and willing to use their method, prefers to operate on cross-sections – at best a sequence of them, on the supposition that a series of still photographs equals a moving picture. Its concerns are best served when it has stopped the stream of history and, in obedience to Emanuel Le Roy Ladurie's powerful advocacy, made it stand still. But time does not stand still and change is the essential experience of man in history. Any form of historical study which, in a supposed search for reality, feels compelled to alter the essence of historical experience, irredeemably perverts that reality. That is not to say that social historians are necessarily wrong to practise their cross-sectional methods; but it is to say that without the overriding control of political history they rapidly move away from writing history at all. For truth to become conveyable there has to be a structure of moving time, and only political history provides that continuously and as a main part of its thinking.

Political history therefore excels at giving attention to real people in real circumstances, and at providing the framework of a motion through time – from conditioning past into unknown (not predetermined) future – which all history needs if it is to reflect and explain reality. However, political history can fulfil its function properly only if it understands the people and the social structures which are politically active, as agents or victims of action. It must therefore absorb as well as criticise the findings of associated forms of historical study, not reject them. Perhaps this seems to reduce such things as the marvels of social history to the role of a service industry. But why not if it serves to improve the sense of historical reality, the grasp of constant change that man both undergoes and actively participates in, seeing that by itself it cannot command that vision?

Ronald Hutton

Political history is the study of the organisation and operation of power in past societies. It is the exhilarating business of observing men and women engaged in what has proved to be the most complex and difficult of human activities, upon which turned not only their own future but the destinies of nations, economies, societies, cultures and faiths. It is a democratising process, laying bare the thoughts and actions of rulers to the descendants of their subjects. More than any other species of history, it involves the destruction of myths, often carefully conceived and propagated. No other variety of historian experiences to such a constant, and awesome, extent, the responsibility of doing justice to the dead.

Political history demands heroic feats of imaginative reconstruction, for the consequences of political decisions are usually much better documented than the decisions themselves. It is also the most protean and least self-sufficient of the varieties of history. The range of political institutions conceivable by human beings and the variety of individual reactions to the demands of holding power both appear remarkably limited. In this sense, politics is one of the most static and timeless of human activities. What has changed constantly has been the ideological context of behaviour, depending in turn upon the evolution of morality, technology, education, religion, patterns of wealth and international relations. Without the best possible understanding of that context, the work of the political historian is futile; if politics is the art of the possible, then past politics cannot be evaluated without an appreciation of what was possible to the participants.

The perception of how to achieve this has itself altered significantly in recent years. Most political histories used to revolve around constitutional documents, accompanied by a political pedigree attached to each. During the past three decades, it has become more usual to concentrate upon the relationship between political and other forms of activity in a given society. Movements in population, prices and rents, local topography and the nature of court or of popular cultures have all become areas of concern to political historians.

Not every period, of course, is equally promising to every variety of investigator. The sixteenth and seventeenth centuries have been called a 'Dark Age' for economic historians. The sources for ancient Egypt reward students of art and social development more than those of political affairs. A case can be made for representing Tudor and Stuart England as one of those sections of time particularly attractive to the political historian. It was the age during which political and religious power in this nation was embodied in more or less the same institutions which contain it at the present. Its events were extremely dramatic and continue to arouse interest in the public and controversy among scholars. Enough evidence for its political affairs has survived to make possible the investigation of many aspects of them with some hope of finding answers.

22

Furthermore, governments had not then mastered the art of destroying compromising documents. The most spectacular illustration of this fact is probably the fate of the secret treaty which Charles II signed with France in 1670, containing matter which might, if published, have toppled his monarchy. His secretary during the negotiations, Sir Thomas Clifford, was allowed to take home with him not merely the English copy but all the working papers for the negotiations themselves. And at his home, Ugbrooke Park in Devon, they have remained ever since.

Finally, it should be said that political activity itself has come to seem more, rather than less, significant as a result of its relation to other aspects of the past. Attempts to portray the English Civil War as a social conflict have failed, and it is once again viewed primarily as a political disaster. Local studies of the English Reformation are revealing how much religious change depended upon the policy of the central government. War, the most dramatic form of politics, is increasingly recognised as a potent factor in social and economic change. While political affairs can never be divorced from their context, they very often possess a momentum and logic of their own, which alter the context itself. The modern study of political history hinges upon this dynamic interaction.

Roy Foster

In the nineteen-sixties, when the world seemed young, one used to hear it said that *'everything* is politics'. It might appear ironic that at that very time an approach to political history was first being advanced which seemed to limit the parameters of the subject to the preoccupations of expert practitioners who had more in common with their collusive opponents within the charmed circle, than with anyone outside it – least of all their nominal supporters. Tactics, rhetoric and a common language, not to mention a common desire to evade 'democracy', mattered far above 'issues'.

This was the approach that received classic exposition in Maurice Cowling's brilliant introduction to *1876, Disraeli, Gladstone and Revolution*: a disquisition which some consider his most lucid (or even his last lucid) piece of historical writing. Seven years later, the coruscating Book One of A. B. Cooke's and J. R. Vincent's *The Governing Passion* advanced a series of structural generalisations about late Victorian political practice which aroused in book reviewers the sort of moral fury not seen since Tawney's and Trevor-Roper's storm over the gentry. There were those who claimed the fashion had peaked and declined by 1980; but it should be noted that one of the latest volumes in the Fontana History of England, Michael

Bentley's *Politics without Democracy 1815–1914* (1984) explicitly follows the traditions of 'exploring perception and preoccupation in British government' rather than 'what actually happened'. Does this indicate that what was initially decried as a microscopically mandarin approach to political history can, first, be applied to general considerations across an entire century; and, second, be made palatable to the general reader?

I think it does; and, further, that those who dismiss 'high-political history' as restricted to what Sir Stafford Northcote wrote or did not write to Lord Cranbrook on a certain date, miss the real significance of the bracing air and light let in by the sceptical excavations of tomb-like Victorian archives begun twenty-odd years ago. The frame of reference within which modern British political historiography operates was created not only by the meticulous landscaping of Gash, Hanham and Pelling, but also by the slashing billhook of Namier – whose interests, more than anyone's, saw political history as comprehended by the study of psychology, intellect and culture. And if political history is to be written as the re-creation of a political culture, it necessarily involves emphasising what people thought they were doing, and why they thought they wanted to do it, as much as the actual (often unintended) outcome of their actions. There is good reason therefore why the work of political historians should concentrate on the intentions and preoccupations of politicians at least as much as on the events of politics. This can hold good for 'popular' politics as well as parliamentary studies. And much recent work shows an encouraging tendency to follow the trend.

This approach may not lend itself easily to the comfortable generalisations which lubricate first-year survey courses. But it need not – indeed, it should not – make redundant the large-scale theme or the grand theory. Marxians oddly shy away from the history of parliamentary politics, but there should be no need for them to do so. If 'social' and 'economic' history is to be seen as more relevant than political history, this can only imply an extremely limited conception of society and economics; and the preoccupations of high political historians, no less than those of E. P. Thompson or Eric Hobsbawm, represent a reaction against the flaccid evangelicalism and complacent compartmentalisations of the 'Oxford History' approach.

In Britain more than elsewhere, the study of élite political behaviour is curiously seen as an élitist preoccupation. One reason may be because of the rather touching identification whereby some historians adopt the politics of the people they write about. There is also another, more subtle, process whereby historians of politics, like most historians, tend to become pessimistic with age; and in their case a pessimistic predisposition can appear to present itself as a sympathy with the combined sleight-of-hand and stasis which characterises British conservatism. But Salisbury and Balfour agreed with Marx in taking class conflict as the basic axiom of political confrontation. And a consciousness that the political culture of modern Britain is too rich, too dense, too stable and too complicated to be dismissed as a superstructural trimming is surely consistent with all but the most reductionist historical theory. A. J. P. Taylor's gadfly virtuosity notwithstanding, connoisseurs of contingency need not necessarily deny the relevance of large patterns.

Nor does the stringency and scepticism of the new political history exclude the traditional format of biography – as some of us have tried to show. Much as Cowling, Cooke, Vincent and Andrew Jones explored specific political crises by conflating evidence from numerous archives, reanimating the immediacy of contemporary preoccupations, and reconstructing the density of day-to-day action, the modern political biographer can be liberated from adherence to the law-tablets of family papers alone. Political actors can be put in context by comparative use of sources, as well as by being placed in a structure of action which refuses to take for granted the assumptions assiduously marketed in laundered speeches and pious memorials. One reason why this is increasingly possible is because the audience has been educated to expect it, by works that have refused to take refuge in begged questions and well-wishing evasions. To the argument that this has meant restricting high political history to high professionals, Bentley's textbook provides the most recent and most cogent answer and it can also be met by citing the first volume of Richard Shannon's marvellously rich and probing life of Gladstone. The preoccupations of such historians may be as easily described as intellectual or psychological as political; they are nonetheless working in a tradition of demanding enquiry which, because less currently fashionable than other avenues, has not yet had its critical due.

John Turner

Arthur Balfour, asked in December 1917 what Britain's war aims should be, replied that this was 'a problem in which I take no very great interest because, as it seems to me, there is not the slightest difficulty in defining what ends we want to achieve. . . . The real difficulty is to find out how far we shall be able to attain them . . . '. This caused some exasperation – as Foreign Secretary he was paid a handsome salary to take an interest in war aims – but political historians ought to sympathise. What we are trying to do seems easy enough to define: politics is about getting and using power in society – or, in the words of the eminent American political scientist Harold Lasswell, settling 'who gets what; when and how' – and we are here to write the history of politics. Whether we can ever succeed is another matter.

Most political historians emphasise the 'how' in Lasswell's aphorism, and in modern British history this almost always means the party system. The state is the most visible centre of power in Britain, and for two centuries politicians have kept control of it through political parties. So historians examine the structure and working of parties: the anatomy and physiology of power in British society. Party history is remarkably eclectic. Practitioners of 'high politics' calendar the letters of the 'fifty or sixty politicians in conscious tension with one another whose accepted authority constituted political leadership'. At the other, 'low' end of the scale the learned journals are full of Tory Party smoking concerts and the assumed second preferences of Liberal voters in rural constituencies in the 1920s. Here, on the face of it, is a discipline brimming with good ideas.

On the face of it, so it is – up to a point. But there is still a lot more 'conscious tension' than actual cooperation between exponents of high and low politics. Some of this is political partisanship: in the Blue corner, Anthony Trollope, high politics and Sir Keith Joseph, in the Red corner, *The Ragged Trousered Philanthropists* and their past and present friends. Some of it is simply habit, and bad habit at that. Biographies look at the social phenomena of politics through the eyes of Westminster politicians. Students of low politics ignore the mental world of Westminster and Whitehall, which explains so much, for example, of the 'reformism' of working-class politics in the twentieth century.

But even if party historians of different sorts could get their act together, party history should never stand for the whole of political history. Let us leave out the exercise of power in society which does not substantially involve the state – little matters like the power of employer over employee and the power of men over women. We are still left with questions about state and society which cannot be understood in party terms. Ralph Miliband in his study of *The State in Capitalist Society* (1969) argues that the state and the holders of economic power prop each other up – the state's power is used in the interests of one class. Party competition, he claims, has made not a jot of difference to this. Nor do we have to go to Marxist fundamentalism to find cases where party history simply will not do. What of politics in wartime, when normal party functions are suspended or greatly modified?

This brings us back to Mr Balfour's irritating levity. War aims mattered in 1917 not because of their effect on the military or diplomatic outcome of the War, but because the government was afraid that the working class would down tools without some good reason for going on. In 1917 discontented Russian workers had taken Russia out of the war and destroyed the old order in the process. So the making of diplomatic policy becomes a subject for the political historian, alongside the party-political struggle. It does not stop there. Social policy in wartime – the making of the Ministry of Health and the beginning of the housing programme – was a weapon in a political struggle between the government and the labour movement for the allegiance of newly enfranchised working-class voters. Direct government intervention in industrial relations protected not only the war effort but also the existing structure of industrial ownership. All this is political; and if it is political in wartime, it is political in peacetime too, and a proper subject for political history.

What is political history? Almost anything you can think of, and probably much that you can't. Write it at your peril.

Kenneth O. Morgan

'Where does power lie and how can it be acquired by the workers?' Thus Aneurin Bevan's definition of the purpose of the politician. For the political historian, concerned with the less glamorous task of description rather than prescription, the object might rather be defined as 'Where does power lie in any given society, what balance of forces affects its operation, and how can its nature be understood and explained?' For many years after 1945, political history was derided as old-fashioned, unadventurous, more superficial than newer disciplines such as social or intellectual history. But it never disappeared as a central preoccupation of historians, whatever their area of research, medieval or modern. Indeed, in the 1980s the prestige of political history seems to be restored. Witness the new emphasis placed by scholars such as Hobsbawm or Stedman Jones on political ideas and strategies in the history of the British working class from the Chartist period onwards.

One reason for the near-contempt with which political history was often regarded in the post-1945 period lay in the narrowness of its definition. Political history, indeed, is far more than the mere record of institutional development. The history of the Liberal or Conservative Parties after 1867 is far more than just the organis-ational story of the National Liberal Federation, the National Union or Central Office. Similarly the Labour Party was much more substantial than merely the sum of the ILP, the Fabians and a multitude of trade unions. Political history, too, is not simply 'high politics', valuable though this method, adopted by several Cambridge historians, has been. To see politics as consisting essentially of the introverted activities of a small élite of governors, operating on the basis of rhetoric or manoeuvre, leads inexorably to the elimination of consideration of policies or programmatic change, and to a failure to link the role of ministers, party *apparatchiks* or civil servants to the wider community of which they formed a part. Political history, too, transcends sheer biography. It is concerned with groups, patterns, collective harmonies and conflicts, continuities and disjunctures. Certainly, it goes far beyond administrative history – an important genre of inquiry which cannot confront the major questions about the mobilisation of power and its translation into decision-making. Political history means the reinterpreting of any given unit or society – a town, a region, a people, a state or an international community – in terms of how power is sought, exercised, challenged, abused or denied.

In terms of my own recent writing, the history of the Attlee government of 1945–51 affords an admirable case-study for the examination of political history as a concept. Of course, one must study the Labour Cabinet ministers in depth and detail, to uncover how policy was framed and executed. Also vital are the relations of ministers to other elements within the Labour movement, the parliamentary party, the trade unions, the machine, ordinary party workers, as well as the pressures imposed from without by largely hostile financial institutions, the administrative structure, the press and other organs of opinion. Internal British political history between 1945 and 1951 also cannot be understood without exploring the role of external forces, political, financial and military. The revamping of the Labour government's policies and priorities in the light of the Cold War, the rise of a multi-racial Commonwealth, the economic, commercial and territorial vacuums created in the world ravaged by six years of total war – all these form part of the study of the Attlee government, too.

But there is more to it even than that. Political debate and change – or lack of it – between 1945 and 1951 were also a reflection of intense social and demographic upheaval after the war and the pre-war slump; the restructuring of the components of the old working- and middle-class base; the shifts of economic activity in the regions of England, in Wales and in Scotland; the transformation of work and of leisure; upheavals in family life; racial, sexual and generational transformation. Politics also reflected, and were influenced by, the expectations and disappointments that marked literature and the arts after 1945. Finally, the historian should not ignore the evidence, however impressionistic and intangible, of changes in the public mood or the national psychology, those subtle modulations that led from the passion for egalitarianism and planning in 1945 to new concern for individual release and freedom from controls, rationing and the servile state. The political history of Britain between 1945 and 1951, then, demands an examination of an entire, complex, turbulent society, viewed from the perspective of the operations and dimensions of power. It is in the interaction of a huge variety of political, socio-economic, cultural and psychological forces that the nature of political change can be assessed. And the materials that the historian uses – public and private MSS and printed sources, the press, novels, radio and films, oral tradition and folk memory – should reflect this variety. To adopt a post-war election slogan, never neglect to 'Ask your Dad' (or Mum).

Finally, political history should never be unduly rationalist. To assess the work of the 1945–51 Labour government, or any other group of politicians, in terms of academic logic or a timeless scale of values is a distortion of events. The historian, after all, is a comfortable, middle-class individual cocooned in his or her study or library, meditating in leisured tranquillity on the crisis that engulfed former men and women in public life. He should never forget the pressures of time and circumstances which inexorably shaped the reactions of harassed politicians. They were not concerned with proclaiming universally valid truths, but with reconciling, managing, muddling through, relating their principles to the real, ravaged, terrifying world as they faced it in 1945. It might help if the historian himself or herself has had first-hand acquaintance of the current political world. As always, experience (including of the passion, anger, nobility and squalor that envelop political activity) is a priceless guide. A political historian who writes donnishly, patronisingly, like a grandee on the saluting base, seriously misinterprets the nature of past politics.

FURTHER READING

Addison, P., *The Road to 1945* (London, 1975); Bentley, M., *Politics without Democracy* (London, 1984); Bloch, M., *The Historian's Craft* (Manchester, 1954); Clarke, P. F., *Liberals and Social Democrats* (Cambridge, 1978); Cooke, A. B. and Vincent, J., *The Governing Passion* (Brighton, 1974); Cowling, M., *Disraeli, Gladstone and Revolution* (Cambridge, 1967); *The Impact of Labour* (Cambridge, 1971); Earl, D. C., *The Moral and Political Tradition of Rome* (London, 1967); Elton, G. R., *Political History: Principles and Practice* (New York, 1970); Foster, R. F., *Lord Randolph Churchill: A Political Life* (Oxford, 1981); Hanham, H. J., *Elections and Party Management:*

Politics in the Time of Disraeli and Gladstone (Harlow, 1959); Hexter, J. H., *Doing History* (Bloomington, Indiana, 1968); Hobsbawm, E. J., *Labouring Men* (London, 1964); *Worlds of Labour* (London, 1984); Jackson, G., *Historian's Quest* (New York, 1969); Lasswell, H., *Politics: Who gets What, When, How* (New York, 1936); Lindblom, C., *Politics and Markets* (New York, 1977); Millar, F., *The Emperor in the Roman World* (London, 1977); Syme, R., *The Roman Revolution* (Oxford, 1939); Wirgzubski, C., *Libertas as a Political Idea at Rome* (Cambridge, 1950); Wiseman, T. P. (ed.), *Roman Political Life 90 BC– AD 69* (Exeter, 1985).

THE CONTRIBUTORS

G. R. Elton is Professor of English Constitutional History at the University of Cambridge. His most influential book is *The Tudor Revolution in Government* (Cambridge, 1953), and his most recent, *Which Road to the Past? Two Views of History* (with R. W. Fogel) (New Haven, 1983).

Roy Foster is Reader in Modern History at Birkbeck College, University of London. His forthcoming books on Ireland include *Nationalism and Popular Protest in Ireland* (Cambridge) and the authorised biography of W. B. Yeats.

Ronald Hutton is Lecturer in History at the University of Bristol and author of *The Restoration: A Political and Religious History of England, 1658–1667* (Oxford, 1985).

K. O. Morgan is Fellow and Praelector, The Queen's College, Oxford, and his most recent book is *The Oxford Illustrated History of Britain* (Oxford, 1984).

John Turner is Lecturer in History at Royal Holloway and Bedford New College, University of London, and editor of *Businessmen in Politics* (London, 1984).

T. P. Wiseman is Professor of Classics at the University of Exeter and author of *Catullus and his World* (Cambridge, 1985).

3. WHAT IS
ECONOMIC HISTORY . . . ?

A simple study of the economic aspects of society? History
with the people left out? Arid quantification? Aggregate
history? Or the study of the essential motivating force of
society? What is economic history?

D. C. Coleman

It is not difficult to concoct brief definitions of economic history; but
nor is it very rewarding. It is easy enough to say that it is the study of
the economic aspects of societies in the past; the history of the
economic use of resources – land, labour and capital; or the
examination of the past performance of economies. One can try to
impart a less impersonal flavour by claiming that it is concerned
with how people lived most of their lives, how many were born and
died, how they earned and spent, worked and played. Such
variants, however, reveal little more than the definition which once
said simply that it was the sort of history which required a
knowledge of economics (which is true); though they are an
advance on that which defined an economic historian as one who
wrote as little history as possible for as much money as possible
(which is fun but untrue).

None of these indicates in what ways economic history is
significantly different from more orthodox varieties of history. And
that is what matters. Because economic history asks economic
questions – be they about the demand and supply of goods and
services, about costs of production, levels of income, the distribution of wealth, the volume and direction of investment, or the
structure of overseas trade – it inevitably deals with large numbers,
with aggregates. This does not mean that it deals only with
aggregates – but more of that anon. Insofar as it does it has to
contend with the task of identifying and measuring forces normally
outside the conscious control of single, individual actors. This
causes much trouble to traditional historians. They, it has been
recently said, 'reject the concept of forces as identifiable agents
creating or conditioning historical events'. If economic historians
took that line it is difficult to see how they could possibly enquire
into such respectable historical topics as, to give a few local
examples, Tudor inflation, Victorian population growth, or the

long-running deficit on Britain's visible balance of commodity trade. Because economic history asks these sorts of questions about these sorts of topics certain other consequences follow. First, those who tackle such problems must have some competence in the statistical handling of measurable variables. Second, they need to understand and be able to use the relevant body of economic theory.

At this point difficulties arise for the economic historians themselves, about such definitions of method. For it is by no means clear what are the relevant, or at any rate useful, bits of economic theory. Economists come and go, usually in happy ignorance of history, and so do their theories. The latter are based upon assumptions which may or may not be true for a particular historical place or time. Over large stretches of the historian's territory quantitative data suitable for the testing of models based upon such theories is often either defective or merely non-existent. Furthermore, the historical economic phenomena to be examined have no existence independent of the social, political, cultural, religious and physical environment in which they occurred. Therefore economic history has both to make up its own theories for testing and also to ask other sorts of questions and use other sorts of methods. It may draw upon different social sciences, for example social anthropology, but pertinent answers are commonly to be found by using the traditional methods of historical scholarship. At these crucial points economic history deals with individuals and groups in society. It concerns itself with particular businessmen or companies, with those who influenced or carried out economic policy, with pressure groups or, administrative entities: thus, with Edward III or Lord Nuffield, with Peel or Keynes, with the medieval manor, the economic views of Protestant Dissenters, or with the TUC. In seeking answers to historical questions in these areas the use of counterfactual propositions involving economic models and statistical manipulation is of very limited value, when not either inappropriate or even impossible.

Economic history has many affinities with what in the eighteenth century was called 'philosophical' or 'conjectural' history, which is not surprising as Adam Smith practised that sort of history while laying down the bases for the study of what he and his contemporaries called political economy and what we have come to call economics. Today the pursuit of economics might well benefit from more of Smith's awareness of history. Economic history itself, however, cannot proceed without using the divergent techniques of both the economist and the historian. And that makes it no soft option.

Roderick Floud

Historians, like politicians, often think that the purpose of economic life is production. It is not; we make and sell not as an end in itself but in order to consume. Through the centuries, men and women have worked for themselves or for others in order to exchange what they have produced for goods and services which they desire.

It follows that the primary aim of economic history is to describe their success in this task and to analyse the different means which they have used. In practice, since no economic system yet devised and put into practice has succeeded in eliminating poverty and disease from the population of the world, the economic historian has the sad task – like that of the 'dismal science' of economics – of describing various levels of failure.

Given this task, it is no accident that the most sustained controversy in British economic history, paralleled in the history of other nations, is that about the standard of living of the population during industrialisation. The standard of living, the level of success or failure which people achieve in fulfilling their desire to consume, is the fundamental measure of the efficiency and equity of an economic system such as slavery, capitalism or communism and of the level of resources and technology which the people of that system have available to them.

Because the standard of living is so fundamental, it is important that we should measure it well. Economic historians have tended to seek simple solutions to this problem, measuring for example the value of national income per head. While such monetary measures are valuable components of living standards, they are not the whole story. Individuals, and whole societies, have placed value on many things other than money incomes; they have valued good health, leisure, military display or long life and have been prepared to trade off such desires against higher money incomes. Moreover, most societies have been very unequal; economic power over men, machines and the results of their work has been in the hands of a few, so that average national income tells us little about the nature of life in a society.

The recognition that this is so has increasingly led economic historians into areas of political, social and intellectual history. The structure of political power and the legal system determine rights to property, to ownership of land and other resources and to the risks and rewards of economic enterprise. Social customs not only shape economic desires but also constrict economic activity, for example in concepts of what is 'women's work' and what 'men's'. Ideologies such as *laisser-faire* or monetarism shape economic policy.

The need to use new and more comprehensive ways of under-standing human behaviour in the past also lies behind current efforts to integrate demography with economic history. The study of such basic decisions as whether to marry or to have a child cannot sensibly be divorced from the study of the resources of the household and the work and living patterns of the society. Health, the length of life and disease, and their interaction with the incomes which people can earn, are also important and the attempt to study them has shaped my own recent research; I am using measurements of the heights of hundreds of thousands of men in the past as a measure of their health, strength and standard of living.

My emphasis on the primacy of measuring and understanding living standards in the past does not rule out the study of production. The organisation of production – whether in farm, workshop or factory – and the technology which was used, has been the traditional subject of enquiry for economic historians. This is reasonable, particularly in the study of societies in which work was life, since there was little time or opportunity for education or leisure. Moreover, the genesis and achievement of technological change remains one of the greatest puzzles of economics and economic history. It is important, however, that the study of machines should not obscure the study of man.

If we are to study man, then we have to accept that we must study men and women in the mass. Although economic history has some heroes – inventors or traders – it is concerned essentially with the behaviour of groups, with generalisation and therefore with theory. Economic history is thus inevitably a social science, applying the methods of economics, statistics, sociology and demography to the study of the past. It is also an essential component of the study of contemporary society, a bridge in both directions between the present and the past.

T. C. Barker

The question 'what is economic history?', was much easier to answer a generation ago than it is today. Few people then doubted that economic history included social history as well. Economic changes did not occur in isolation but were related to their effects upon mankind. There were specialists in the economic history of earlier periods, such as Eileen Power and R. H. Tawney, but most interest was focused upon the industrial revolution and its effects. This was popular with evening classes as well as at university, where it was usually taught as a subsidiary subject. Students devoured the writing of the Hammonds and G. D. H. Cole who made the most of what they saw as the disadvantages of unfettered private enterprise. To this extent the subject provided ammunition for those in favour of the welfare state. Others, notably Clapham and Ashton, interpreted industrialisation in a very different way. Stimulating debates arose. After the war the subject grew rapidly: university departments were formed; more research was set in train.

More research, however, meant more specialisation. The subject began to fragment as particular areas, such as population growth, finance, transport, towns and individual businesses came to be more carefully investigated. Specialised groups and specialised journals appeared. Much of this new work was above the heads of undergraduates, let alone evening students. There was more and more reading to be done. In any case, the welfare state had arrived and new concerns were at hand, not least the means to maintain it.

During the 1960s, while the going got harder, an epidemic of this more mathematical approach to history spread from the United States, where economic history is usually taught in economics departments. This appealed to those economic historians in Britain who had been trained primarily as economists, but not to those whose background was in history. Even many of the former, however, came to see that the newcomers often showed scant regard for the reliability of the numerical sources on which their work was based, and, indeed, often did not relate it to more traditional sorts of evidence.

On the whole, the New Economic History further diminished the subject's broad appeal. Those who were interested in its more social aspects, presented in easily comprehensible form, tended to gravitate to political history which in the meantime had absorbed these more attractive features of the economic historians' researches. The numbers of 'O' and 'A' Level candidates in economic history, and the membership of the Economic History Society, which had all been growing impressively in the 1950s and 60s, then levelled off. With the subsequent change in the economic climate and the greater appeal of subjects such as social studies at school and law and accounting at university, economic history has been obliged to take serious stock of itself. Specialised research continues but the results selected to appeal to a wide modern audience is giving the subject a new look.

Economic history can still claim to deal with the fundamentals of the past in a way that no other branch of history does. It still provides not only the good mental training provided by other sorts of history, but also the best means of gaining a deeper understanding of the present and present problems. But, to maintain its wide appeal, economic historians are appreciating that they need, today as in the past, to present such basic economic matters as wage and price movements, rates and levels of unemployment, imports and exports, into language which those keen to learn can readily comprehend; and, at the same time and more important, to show how people in different sections of society have been affected by them. In practice, this means a greater switch to the social aspects: not the old rag-bag that used to pass for social history but something built up logically upon basic economic foundations. Given this approach, it has been possible to construct new courses dealing with such topics as the growth of leisure and its manifold effects; industrial relations (not just trade union history), and business history: the study of the units, not only in manufacturing industry, which, collectively, generate economic wealth. An economic foundation, too, provides the most useful starting point for any study of the women's movement. Here, as in other interpretations, there is much to be learned from other subjects such as sociology and psychology. Just as the political historians have benefited from many of the economic historians' researches, so the economic historians, in their turn, will gain from findings in other subjects.

In developing these new initiatives, more attention is being paid to the twentieth century. We are all much more interested nowadays not in the great industrial revolution but in Britain's miserable performance since 1945. This is now seen both in terms of these post-war decades and in a longer historical perspective. It is seen, too, in terms of the living conditions of various sections of society, where the post-war years have been far from miserable for most people. Britain's dismal performance has been comparative and here the growth of other countries is being more actively studied, not only Europe, the United States, the Commonwealth and the growth of an interconnected international economy over the past century – all long featured on economic history syllabuses – but also Russia, India and Japan and the growth of Third World countries.

The 'modernisation' of the subject is being much aided by new historical sources. Careful interviews of elderly people, conducted by historians who have gained a good background knowledge from more traditional evidence, can fill many gaps and much enrich our understanding of ordinary folk's social conditions and personal priorities, so often distorted by the writings of leaders and activists.

In the end, history is all of a piece. The different branches approach it from different points of view. Economic history claims that its approach is more fundamental than the others; but for more general appeal, it must continue to relate to current interests as it did earlier in the century with such success.

M. J. Daunton

A cynic might be inclined to enquire 'what *was* economic history?', for the subject is, institutionally at least, in retreat. In many universities, departments of economic history have merged with the history department. The increasing loss of institutional status is largely explained by the coincidence that many professors appointed in the heady days of expansion in the 1960s have retired at a time of cutbacks in the 1980s; but for all that the process does have an intellectual justification.

The initial separation did have its rationale, for many history departments had become introverted and narrow, pursuing the increasingly marginal returns of a particular type of high political history. This justification can no longer be argued. Many historians have researched in the field and published in the *Economic History Review* without any formal connection with the subject. A separate identity is no longer required to protect a neglected area of enquiry and, on the contrary, it is now Departments of Economic History which have become introverted and narrow, pursuing the increasingly marginal returns of a particular type of economic theory. Institutional separation has led to intellectual isolation, and the subject is too important for that.

Economic history is still too dependent upon a theoretical underpinning which makes assumptions about behaviour in the past which were not necessarily present at the time. The dominant concern is the allocation of scarce resources of land, labour and capital, and whether this was done in a manner which produced the most rapid rate of economic growth; the process is usually seen as value-free and lacking in conflict. British industrialists in the late nineteenth century, we are now told, should not be damned for neglecting new techniques of production which were developed in Germany or America, for they were using their resources of labour and capital in a way which produced the highest rate of economic growth which was feasible. The motor of historical change is the movement of resources in response to their relative price: if skilled labour is cheap relative to capital, it pays to maintain handicraft methods of production; and if capital is cheap relative to skilled labour, it makes sense to adopt mass production. But was this really how the societies operated? It depends upon whether the skilled labourers were unionised, and whether their organisations were brought into the political system: the relationship between the 'labour aristocrats' of British industry and the Liberal party was very different from the situation in Germany or America. It also depends upon whether the employers wished to wrest control of the shop floor from the skilled men and their unions and to erect a new system of discipline and labour relations. The American employers were more willing to adopt the necessary aggressive response than their British counterparts, for reasons which have much to do with their relative social standing and political freedom. The narrowly economic soon gives way to the political and the social.

My own recent work on housing in Victorian cities has followed precisely this approach of integrating economic, social, and political history. Of course, it was necessary to analyse the operation of the land market, the structure of the building industry, the source of funds, the course of the building cycle. It was clear, however, that social and political questions were raised. The building cycle entailed periodic gluts and shortages of houses which changed the balance of power between landlords and tenants as they tussled over the level of rents and the collection of arrears. But their relative power might also be determined by the legal system which might give security to the tenants or ease of repossession to the landlords. This was essentially a political question, depending upon the ability of landlords to mobilise and to influence the major parties, and their relationship with other interest groups. The political analysis must then be brought to bear upon the economics of housing, for the failure of the landlords to secure redress of their grievances, as the burden of local taxation mounted and the tenants won greater protection, eroded the profitability of investment in housing. This might in turn force the state to intervene to provide public housing. Any attempt to separate economic, social, and political history would have produced an incomplete picture.

I am not arguing that economic history is unimportant; on the contrary I believe that it is an essential part of any understanding of the past, provided that it is not treated in isolation. It is now 'mainstream' historians who have the more eclectic and imaginative response to the past, with their willingness to bring a variety of methodologies to bear. Economic historians can only lose by cutting themselves off in separate departments or courses. Students may still take A-level papers or undergraduate degrees in economic history without being aware of the wider political or cultural context, which is not only limiting for them; it also has the unfortunate consequence that teachers of history are encouraged to minimise the economic history component of their courses. How is it possible to understand the development of modern British political history without considering, say, the emergence of the business corporation and a managerial class, or the impact of work practices upon the structure of the working class? Anything which permits historians to exclude such themes must be avoided, and this must rest upon a willingness of economic historians to move from their introverted concerns to a full engagement in the wider debate.

N. F. R. Crafts

Economic history can be thought of as a search for understanding of the nature of economic activity in the past. Such study is intrinsically rewarding but also can be useful in shedding light on questions of relevance to economic policy makers. Indeed it might be argued that economic history should be as much a standard part of the training of professional economists as is statistics.

Major practitioners of economic history at least since Clapham have recognised that inevitably there is a considerable element of quantification in the subject. In future, students familiar with the use of computers before they become undergraduates will expect and be able to develop skills in the quantitative analysis of historical events. What is much less generally accepted in Britain (though things are rather different in the USA) is that serious progress in economic history requires the skills both of economics and history. A prejudice of mine is that a joint degree in history and economics is a better preparation for the aspiring economic historian than the usual British approach of a degree in 'Economic History'.

These points can be developed by looking briefly at recent research in two important areas, namely, the growth of the economy at the time of the Industrial Revolution and unemployment in Britain between the wars.

Our view of the Industrial Revolution depends greatly on the quantitative information available on the rate of economic growth. It is no exaggeration to say that the publication of Deane and Cole's *British Economic Growth, 1688–1959* transformed the historiography of the Industrial Revolution. Recent developments have led to major refinements and modifications to Deane and Cole's work. The upshot of this research is to show that prior to 1820 the British economy grew slowly and that the British Industrial Revolution consisted of a rapid change in the structure of employment rather than dramatic productivity growth in the economy as a whole.

It is revealing then to ask on what this progress has been based. The answer is that it has depended on the use of a wide range of historical, economic and quantitative skills by many individuals. Thus, painstaking work with burial records and regression analysis enabled Lindert to show that Gregory King's England was less agricultural than used to be thought; detailed use of source material and national income accounting methodology produced Feinstein's estimates of capital formation; a sophisticated computer model involving back projection provided Wrigley and Schofield's convincing estimates of population growth in the pre-Census era; the theory of index numbers helped Harley to show that industrial production only grew slowly before 1815; and my application of the economist's techniques of demand analysis gave new results on agricultural growth.

Changing fashions in economic theory have led economists to new interpretations of the persistently high levels of unemployment in the 1920s and 1930s. Benjamin and Kochin have claimed that there was a high 'natural rate' of unemployment, much of which was voluntary and induced by over-generous unemployment benefits. Such a claim has obvious policy relevance today but has been strongly and effectively criticised by economic historians like Hatton.

The debate has several important lessons about economic history. First, a detailed knowledge of the period and historical sources is exceptionally useful in assessing the idea that unemployment was voluntary; a historian familiar with the evidence of much long-duration unemployment and with contemporary accounts such as that of Bakke has a headstart. Second, such expertise is not sufficient because the telling criticisms of Benjamin and Kochin have also required econometric sophistication. Third, a marriage of historical knowledge and familiarity with modern economists' empirical work also serves to advance the discussion. In a recent paper I demonstrated the extent of long-duration unemployment, indicated that modern studies do not find evidence that such unemployment is induced by benefits and also pointed to the weakness of trade unionism in the 1930s, on account of which standard economic models would lead one to expect a much lower 'natural rate' of unemployment in the 1930s than in the 1970s.

In other words the expertise of an economic historian tends to produce better economic history than results from economists' unaided efforts; but the economic historian requires skills in economics, history and quantitative methods. Economic history can and should make a positive and important contribution to policy debates.

FURTHER READING

Barker, T. C., Campbell, R. H., Matthais, P. and Yamey, B. S., *Business History* (third edition, London, 1984); Chaloner, W. H. and Richardson, R. C. (compilers), *Bibliography of British Economic and Social History* (Manchester, 1984); Coleman, D. C., *History and the Economic Past* (Oxford, forthcoming); Court, W. H. B., *Scarcity and Choice in History* (London, 1970); Crafts, N. F. R., *British Economic Growth during the Industrial Revolution* (Oxford, 1985); Edwards, R., *Contested Terrain: The Transformation of the Workplace in the*

Twentieth Century (London, 1979); Floud, R. C. and McCloskey, D. N. (eds), *The Economic History of Britain since 1700* (Cambridge, 1981); Fogel, R. W. and Engerman, S. L., *Time on the Cross* (London, 1974); McClelland, *Causal Explanation and Model Building in History, Economics and the New Economic History* (New York, 1975); Matthews, R. C. O. *et al*, British Economic Growth, 1856–1973 (Stanford, 1982); Price, R., *Masters, Unions and Men: Work Control in Building and the Rise of Labour* (Cambridge, 1980); Rosenberg, N., *Perspectives on Technology* (Cambridge, 1976); Thompson, P., *The Voice of the Past: Oral History* (Oxford, 1978); Williamson, J. G., *Did British Capitalism Breed Inequality?* (London, 1985); Wrigley, E. A. and Schofield, R. S., *The Population History of England, 1541–1871* (London, 1981).

THE CONTRIBUTORS

T. C. Barker is Professor Emeritus of Economic History, University of London, and the author of books on urbanisation, transport and business history.

D. C. Coleman is Professor Emeritus of Economic History, University of Cambridge and author of *The Economy of England, 1450–1750* (Oxford, 1977).

N. F. R. Crafts is C.U.F. Lecturer in Economics at Oxford University and author of *British Economic Growth during the Industrial Revolution* (Oxford, 1985).

M. J. Daunton is Lecturer in Economic History at University College London. His most recent book is *His Royal Mail: Britain's Post Office since 1840* (London, 1985).

Roderick Floud is Professor of Modern History at Birkbeck College, University of London, and editor of *The Economic History of Britain since 1700* (Cambridge, 1981).

4. WHAT IS
SOCIAL HISTORY . . . ?

*A new form of antiquarianism? Celebrating experience at
the expense of analysis? The sort of history Socialists write?
Mobilising popular enthusiasm? A portmanteau term? Or
offering the best opportunity for writing total history? What
is social history?*

Raphael Samuel

Ever since its elevation to the status of a discipline, and the
emergence of a hierarchically organised profession, history has
been very largely concerned with problematics of its own making.
Sometimes it is suggested by 'gaps' which the young researcher is
advised by supervisors to fill; or by an established interpretation
which, iconoclastically, he or she is encouraged to challenge.
Fashion may direct the historians' gaze; or a new methodology may
excite them; or they may stumble on an untapped source. But
whatever the particular focus, the context is that enclosed and
esoteric world in which research is a stage in the professional career;
and the 'new' interpretation counts for more than the substantive
interest of the matter in hand.

Social history is quite different. It touches on, and arguably helps
to focus, major issues of public debate, as for example on British
national character or the nature of family life. It mobilises popular
enthusiasm and engages popular passions. Its practitioners are
counted in thousands rather than hundreds – indeed tens of
thousands if one were to include (as I would) those who fill the
search rooms of the Record Offices, and the local history rooms of
the public libraries, documenting family 'roots'; the volunteer
guides at the open-air museums; or the thousands of railway
fanatics who spend their summer holidays acting as guards or
station staff on the narrow gauge lines of the Pennines and North
Wales. Social history does not only reflect public interest, it also
prefigures and perhaps helps to create it. Thus 'Victorian Values'
were being rehabilitated by nineteenth-century enthusiasts for a
decade or more before Mrs Thatcher appropriated them for her
Party's election platform; while Professor Hoskins' discovery of
'lost' villages, and his celebration of the English landscape anticipated some of the animating sentiments which have made the

conservationist movement a force for planners to reckon with.

As a pedagogic enthusiasm, and latterly as an academic practice, social history derives its vitality from its oppositional character. It prides itself on being concerned with 'real life' rather than abstractions, with 'ordinary' people rather than privileged élites, with everyday things rather than sensational events. As outlined by J. R. Green in his *Short History of the English People* (1874) it was directed against 'Great Man' theories of history, championing the peaceful arts against the bellicose preoccupations of 'drum-and-trumpet' history. In its inter-war development, represented in the schools by the Piers Plowman text-books, and in the universities by Eileen Power's *Medieval People* and the work of the first generation of economic historians, it evoked the human face of the past – and its material culture – against the aridities of constitutional and administrative development. The *Annales* school in France called for the study of structure and process rather than the analysis of individual events, emphasising the grand permanencies of geography, climate and soil.

Urban history, pioneered as a cottage industry by H. J. Dyos in the 1960s, and labour history, as redefined in E. P. Thompson's *Making of the English Working Class*, was a protest against the routinisation and narrowing of economic history, together with (in the case of Thompson) sideswipes at the invading generalities of the sociologists.

Social history owes its current prosperity, both as a popular enthusiasm and as a scholarly practice, to the cultural revolution of the 1960s, and reproduces – in however mediated a form – its leading inspirations. One is dealing here with homologies rather than influences or, in any publicly acknowledged sense, debts, so that any coupling is necessarily speculative and might seem impertinent to the historians concerned. Nevertheless, if only as a provocation and as a way of positioning history within the imaginative complexes of its time, some apparent convergences might be suggested.

The spirit of 1960s social history – tacking in its own way to the 'winds of change' – was pre-eminently a *modernising* one, both chronologically, in the choice of historical subject matter, and methodologically, in the adoption of multi-disciplinary perspectives. Whereas constitutional history had its original heart in medieval studies, and economic history, as it developed in the 1930s and 1940s, was centrally preoccupied with Tudor and Stuart times (the famous controversy on 'The Rise of the Gentry' is perhaps representative), the 'new' social history, first in popular publication in the railway books (as of David and Charles) and later in its academic version, was apt to make its historical homeland in

Victorian Britain, while latterly, in its enthusiasm for being 'relevant' and up-to-date, it has shown a readiness, even an eagerness, to extend its inquiry to the present. Methodologically too, in ways presciently announced at the beginning of the decade in E. H. Carr's *What is History?* the new social history was hospitable to the social sciences, and much of the energy behind the expansion of *Past and Present* – the most ecumenical of the social history journals, and the first to be preoccupied with the inter-relationship of history and 'theory' – came from the discovery of historical counterparts to the categories of social anthropology and sociology: e.g. 'sub-cultures', social mobility, crowd psychology, and latterly gender identities.

One way in which numbers of the new social historians made themselves at home in the past was by projecting modernity backwards, finding anticipations of the present in the past. This seems especially evident in the American version of social history, where modernisation theory is a leading inspiration (Eugen Weber's *Peasants into Frenchmen*, a celebration of the allegedly civilising process, is an accessible and influential example). It can also be seen in the preoccupation with the origins of 'companionate' marriage and the modern family, a work pioneered in a liberal-humanist vein by Lawrence Stone, and in a more conservative one by Peter Laslett and Alan Macfarlane. Keith Thomas' magnificent *Man and the Natural World*, like his earlier *Religion and the Decline of Magic*, though finely honed and attentive to counter-tendencies, might also be said to be structured by a version of modernisation theory documenting the advance of reason and humanity.

The plebeian subject matter favoured by the new social history, corresponds to other cultural manifestations of the 1960s, as for instance 'new wave' British cinema, with its cockney and provincial heroes, 'pop art' with its use of everyday artefacts, or the transformation of a 'ghetto' beat (Liverpool sound) into a national music. Similarly, the anti-institutional bias of the new social history – the renewed determination to write the history of 'ordinary' people as against that of statecraft, could be said to echo, or even, in some small part to be a constituent element in, a much more widespread collapse of social deference, and a questioning of authority figures of all kinds. In another field – that of historical conservation – one could point to the new attention being given to the preservation and identification of vernacular architecture; to the spread of open-air, 'folk', and industrial museums, with their emphasis on the artefacts of everyday life; and on the retrieval and publication of old photographs, with a marked bias towards the representation of scenes from humble life. The democratisation of genealogy, and the remarkable spread of family history societies – a 'grassroots' movement of primary research – could also be said to reflect the egalitarian spirit of the 1960s; a new generation of researchers finds as much delight in discovering plebeian origins as earlier ones did in the tracing of imaginary aristocratic pedigrees.

Another major 1960's influence on the new social history – very different in its origins and effects – was the 'nostalgia industry' which emerged as a kind of negative counterpart, or antiphon, to the otherwise hegemonic modernisation of the time. The animating sentiment – a very opposite of Mr Wilson's 'white heat of modern technology', or Mr Macmillan's 'winds of change' – was a poignant sense of loss, a disenchantment, no less apparent on the Left of the political spectrum than on the Right – with post-war social change. One is dealing here with a whole set of transferences and displacements in which a notion of 'tradition', previously attached to the countryside and disappearing crafts was transposed into an urban and industrial setting.

Automation, electrification and smokefree zones transformed steam-powered factories into industrial monuments. Property restorers, working in the interstices of comprehensive re-development, turned mean streets into picturesque residences – Victorian 'cottages' rather than emblems of poverty, overcrowding and ill-health. The pioneers here were the railway enthusiasts who, in the wake of the Beeching axe and dieselisation, embarked on an extravagant series of rescue operations designed to bring old lines back to life. A little later came the steam traction fanatics; the collectors of vintage fairground engines; and the narrow-boat enthusiasts and canal trippers, bringing new life to disused industrial waterways. Industrial archaeology, an invention of the 1960s, followed in the same track, elevating relics of the industrial revolution, like Coalbrookdale, to the status of national monuments. In another sphere one could point to the proliferation of folk clubs (one of the early components of 1960s 'counter-culture'), and the discovery of industrial folk song, as prefiguring one of the major themes of the new social history: the dignity of labour. Another of its major themes – solidarity – could be said to have been anticipated by that sub-genre of autobiography and sociological enquiry – Hoggart's *Uses of Literacy* (1957) was the prototype – which made the vanishing slum a symbol of lost community.

So far as historical work was concerned, these sentiments crystallised in an *anti-progressive* interpretation of the past, a folkloric enthusiasm for anachronism and survival, and an elegaic regard for disappearing communities. 'Resurrectionism' – rescuing the past from the 'enormous condescension' of posterity, reconstituting the vanished components of 'The World We Have Lost' – became a major impetus in historical writing and research. The dignity of 'ordinary' people could be said to be the unifying theme of this line of historical enquiry and retrieval, a celebration of everyday life, even, perhaps especially, when it involved hardship and suffering.

The general effect of the new social history has been to enlarge the map of historical knowledge and legitimate major new areas of scholarly inquiry – as for example the study of households and kinship; the history of popular culture; the fate of the outcast and the oppressed. It has given a new lease of life to extra-mural work in history, more especially with the recent advent of women's history to which social history has been more hospitable than others. It has built bridges to the popular representation of history on television. In the schools it has helped to produce, or been accompanied by, a very general turn from 'continuous' history to superficially project and topic-based learning – a change whose merits the Minister of Education, as well as others, are now challenging. It has also produced a number of 'do-it-yourself' historical projects, as in local history, labour history, oral history, woman's history, which have taken the production of historical knowledge far outside academically defined fiefs.

The new social history has also demonstrated the usefulness – and indeed the priceless quality – of whole classes of documents which were previously held in low esteem: household inventories as an index of kinship, obligations and ties: court depositions as evidence of sociability; wills and testaments as tokens of religious belief. It is less than a century since a distinguished scholar remarked that no serious historian would be interested in a laundry bill. The publications of the Historical Manuscripts Commission and the patrician collections of 'family' papers which adorn the County Record Offices testify to the representative character of this bias. It is unlikely that even so determined a critic of the new social history as, say, Professor Elton, with his belief that history is 'about government', would want to repeat it today.

Despite the novelty of its subject matter, social history reproduces many of the characteristic biases of its predecessors. It is not difficult to find examples of displaced 'Whig' interpretation in 'modernisation' theory; or the 'idol of origins' in accounts of the rise of the Welfare State or the development of social movements. Social historians – proceeding, as Stubbs recommended a century ago, 'historically' rather than 'philosophically' – are no less susceptible than earlier scholars to the appeals of a commonsense empiricism in which the evidence appears to speak for itself, and explanation masquerades as the simple reproduction of fact. Many too could be said to be influenced, albeit subconsciously, by an aesthetic of 'naive realism' (something to which the present writer pleads guilty) in which the more detailed or 'thick' the description, the more authentic the picture is supposed to be. Social historians are good at amassing lifelike detail – household artefacts, time-budgets, cere- monial ritual: they leave no conceptual space for the great absences, for the many areas where the documentary record is silent, or where the historian holds no more than what Tawney once called 'the thin shrivelled tissue' in the hand.

Social history has the defects of its qualities. Its preference for 'human' documents and for close-up views have the effect of *domesticating* the subject matter of history, and rendering it – albeit unintentionally – harmless. The 'sharp eye for telling detail' on which practitioners pride themselves, the colloquial phrases they delight to turn up, the period 'atmosphere' they are at pains faithfully to evoke, all have the effect of confusing the picturesque and the lifelike with the essence of which it may be no more than a chance appearance (much the same defect can be seen on the 'background' detail of historical romance and costume drama). Whereas political history invites us to admire the giants of the past and even vicariously to share in their triumphs, its majesty reminds us of the heights we cannot scale. Social history establishes an altogether intimate rapport, inviting us back into the warm parlour of the past.

The indulgence which social historians extend towards their subjects, and the desire to establish 'empathy' – seeing the past in terms of its own values rather than those of today, can also serve to flatter our self-esteem, making history a field in which, at no great cost to ourselves, we can demonstrate our enlarged sympathies and benevolence. It also serves to rob history of all its terrors. The past is no longer another country when we find a rational core to seemingly irrational behaviour – e.g. that witchcraft accusations were a way of disburdening a village of superfluous old women; or that printers who massacred cats were engaging in a surrogate for a strike.

The identifications which social history invites – one of its leading inspirations and appeals – also have the effect of purveying symbolic reassurance. It establishes a too easy familiarity, the illusion that we are losing ourselves in the past when in fact we are using it for the projection of ideal selves. Recognising our kinship to people in the past, and tracing, or discovering, their likeness to ourselves, we are flattered in the belief that as the subliminal message of a well-known advert has it, underneath we are all lovable; eccentric perhaps, and even absurd, but large-hearted, generous and frank. Our very prejudices turn out to be endearing – or at any rate harmless – when they are revealed as quintessentially English. The people of the past thus become mirror images – or primitive versions of our ideal selves: the freeborn Englishman, as individualist to the manner born, acknowledging no man as his master, truculent in the face of authority; the companionate family, 'a loved circle of familiar faces', living in nuclear households; the indulgent and affectionate parents, solicitous only for the happiness and well-being of their young. These identifications are almost always – albeit subliminally – self-congratulatory. They involve double misrecognition both of the people of the past and of ourselves, in the first place denying them their otherness, and the specificity of their existence in historical time; in the second reinforcing a sentimental view of ourselves. The imaginary community with the past can thus serve as a comfortable alternative to critical awareness and self-questioning, allowing us to borrow prestige from our adoptive ancestors, and to dignify the present by illegitimate association with the past.

Social history, if it is to fulfil its subversive potential, needs to be a great deal more disturbing. If it is to celebrate a common humanity, and to bring past and present closer together, then it must take some account of those dissonances which we know of as part of our own experience – the fears that shadow the growing up of children, the pain of unrequited love, the hidden injuries of class, the ranklings of pride, the bitterness of faction and feud. Far more weight needs to be given, than the documents alone will yield, to the Malthusian condition of everyday life in the past and to the psychic effects of insecurities and emergencies which we can attempt to document, but which escape the categories of our experience, or the imaginative underpinning of our world view. 'Defamiliarisation', in short, may be more important for any kind of access to the past than a too precipitate intimacy. Perhaps too we might recognise – even if the recognition is a painful one – that there is a profound condescension in the notion of 'ordinary people' – that unified totality in which social historians are apt to deal. Implicitly it is a category from which we exclude ourselves, superior persons if only by our privilege of hindsight. 'There are . . . no masses', Raymond Williams wrote in *Culture and Society*, 'only ways of seeing people as masses'. It is perhaps time for historians to scrutinise the term 'the common people' in the same way.

John Breuilly

Social history is more difficult to define than political or economic or military history. Whereas those terms apply to the history of distinct kinds of activity, the term social covers virtually everything. In fact there have been three very different views about the nature of social history.

The oldest view of social history was that it was the history of manners, of leisure, of a whole range of social activities which were conducted outside political, economic, military and any other institutions which were the concern of specific kinds of history. One problem with this rather residual view of social history was that its domain shrank as historians of women, the family, leisure, education, etc., developed their own fields as distinct disciplines. There was also the danger that these histories could become trivialised by the exclusion of politics, economics or ideas from the activities they were investigating.

In a reaction against this some historians have gone to the other extreme and argued that social history should become the history of society: societal history. The idea is that political, economic, military and other specific types of history each study only one aspect of a society. It is necessary to bring these various types of history together into a single framework if that whole society is to be understood. This is the task of societal history.

There are many difficulties with this view of social history. First, the whole approach is based upon the assumption that there is a society to study. But when we use the term society we do not normally mean a distinct social structure, but rather the inhabitants of a certain territory or the subjects of a particular political authority. It remains to be established whether there is a distinct social structure which shapes the way these people live their lives. There is a danger that this assumption of a single society will be imposed upon the evidence. Thus the assumption that English society was becoming industrial during the nineteenth century, along with various ideas about what a pre-industrial and an industrial society are like, can distract from the proper task of the historian. Instead of describing and analysing specific events, the historian is lured into categorising various elements of 'society' according to where they are located on the path from pre-industrial to industrial. This 'evidence' is then cited in support of the original assumption. The argument is unhistorical, circular and empty of real meaning.

A much more promising way of bringing the different branches of history together into a single framework is to distinguish between different dimensions such as the political, the economic and the ideological. Then one tries to relate these different levels together. Marxist history is the best example of this kind of enterprise. But equally the tradition associated with Max Weber can lead in the same direction although with important differences. In both cases, however, the central concern is no longer with 'society' but rather with other concepts such as 'mode of production' or 'types of legitimate domination'. It makes little sense to call these approaches examples of social or societal history. There may still be the assumption that the ultimate purpose is to understand 'society as a whole' or a 'social formation', but this assumption is not an essential element in these types of history. What is essential is how the different dimensions are defined and then related to the evidence and to one another.

A third view of social history is that it is concerned with experience rather than action. One might argue that people who are wage-earners, parents, citizens, consumers and much else besides must possess some sense of identity which underlies all these particular roles and must experience the world in ways which extend beyond these roles. The job of the social historian is to provide a general understanding not at the level of 'society as whole' but at the level of the individual or the members of particular social groups.

But there are problems with this. All the historian can do is study the records of people's actions in the past which still exist. The temptation to go 'behind' those actions to the 'real' people can lead to unverifiable speculation. It can lead away from the concern with specific events which is the essence of history. Finally it can lead away from the social into the psychological. The recent upsurge of interest in the history of 'everyday life' has sometimes demonstrated these weaknesses when it has sought to go beyond the rather antiquarian pursuit of bits and pieces of 'ordinary life'.

These three views of social history – as a residual history of assorted social activities, as societal history, and as the history of social experience – seem to lead nowhere. Confronted with much of what calls itself social history one might feel inclined to settle for this negative conclusion. But I think that at least for modern history there is a further point to be made.

Modern history has witnessed a dramatic increase in the scale of human activity with the growth in size and importance of markets, firms, states and other institutions. People relate to one another in these institutions with little in the way of a common sense of identity or personal knowledge of one another. The studies of these institutions tend, therefore, to omit a consideration of the ways individuals understand their actions within the institutions. But in the end those understandings determine how the institutions perform. By 'understanding' I do not mean some experience 'behind' what people do, but rather the thinking that directly and immediately informs their actions. It is this which should always be related to the performance of the institution as a whole. For example, the historical study of the 'adaptation' of rural immigrants to urban-industrial life cannot work either at the level of impersonal analysis (how far people adjust to certain 'imperatives' of modernisation) or at the level of individual experience (what it is like to be a rural immigrant). Rather one should look at distinct actions such as job-changing, absenteeism, patterns of settlement and housing use. Then one should ask what sort of thinking it is which gives a sense to these patterns of action as well as what this means for the institution concerned. This is hardly the province of a special sort of history. Rather it involves making every kind of history explicitly confront the social nature of action and institutions. Social history is not a particular kind of history; it is a dimension which should be present in every kind of history.

J. C. D. Clark

What is social history? The question used to be asked differently: what is history *tout court*? Philosophers laboured to defend the viability of 'historical explanation' as such against the claims of the natural or social sciences. Yet practising historians know that history is not one thing, but many things. University history faculties are battlefields where different sorts of history compete for space, each sort equipped with a different methodology and value-system. Social history is a natural loser in such a contest: its nature isn't obvious. In rough but useful terms, politics generates political history, war outlines military history, churchmanship identifies religious history. But 'social history' seems a portmanteau term: 'social' action is too general to define an academic genre. So the debate is partly semantic (shall we call *this* or *that* sort of history 'social'?), partly a search for a Holy Grail (is there a holistic social history which transcends and incorporates everything else?). Despite Harold Perkin's impressive achievement, this last idea hasn't been generally persuasive, any more than Leavis' attempt to turn literary criticism into *the* holistic study in the arts.

Social historians are still divided. So what is the semantic debate? What are the divisions? I must answer for my own field, England between the Restoration and the Reform Bill. First in time, but still influential, were the Fabians and Marxists of the pre-1945 generations: the Webbs, the Hammonds, Wallas, Cole, Laski, Tawney and their modern successors. For them, social history was small-scale economic history: standard of living, enclosures, transport, public health, poor law, the economically-generated categories of 'class', municipal matters, drains. It was worthy, but now seems desperately Attlee-esque. And why was this different from economic history as such? On the basis of their reductionist methodologies, no distinction was possible. Nor was it possible in the work, secondly, of subsequent cohorts of New Left historians writing on radicalism, popular protest, riots, crime, prisons, revolution, 'social control'.

The structure of the argument was the same: Roy Porter's concept of social history in *English Society in the Eighteenth Century* is identical to Christopher Hill's concept of economic history in *Reformation to Industrial Revolution*. R. W. Malcolmson's *Life and Labour in England 1700–1780* still touches its forelock to Marx and Engels. One sense in which this work approaches the holistic is that social history is made to seem the sort of history that socialists write.

The third party in the semantic debate seeks to break this closed shop by building its research on a non-positivist, anti-reductionist methodology. Emancipated from its servitude to economic history, social history might be reformulated as the historical sociology of power, ideology and belief, of structure, cohesion, allegiance, faith and identity as well as of innovation and dissent. If politics and ideology (rather than economics) are used to provide a framework for social history, three things, conventionally ignored, would be placed at the top of the social historian's agenda in 1660–1832: religion; the aristocracy and gentry; the monarchy. Social structure, seen in non-positivist terms, highlights England as an *ancien régime* state, with a dominant Church, a clerical intelligentsia, an élite defined in cultural, not economic, terms, and as a polity from which 'liberal(ism)' and 'radical(ism) as political nouns were appropriately absent. Too often the period still takes its chronology from economic history: 1660–1760 is a desert; 1760 onwards is dominated by a reified Industrial Revolution (with invariable capitals), a category discredited by the 'new' economic history. Church history is still a neglected specialism, like military and naval history; the universities are ignored until the era of reform; studies of the aristocracy and gentry are still mainly studies of landownership.

We all know (after all, J. H. Plumb's generation said so) that England from 1688 was secular, contractarian, Lockeian, a world made safe for bourgeois individualism. The 'new' social history will replace this model with an England distressingly different in its priorities from those of the 1960s intelligentsia, so bridging the adjacent achievements of Laslett, Schochet, Thomas, Perkin, Moore. It seems easier for outsiders, free from our parochial commitments: Alan Heimert, Bernard Semmel, Gordon Schochet, Alan Gilbert, Rhys Isaac on religion and society put their English colleagues to shame. Is this social history? Partly the question is semantic, but more is at stake in the clash of materialist and idealist methodologies, and the cultural hegemonies that academic debates echo. Semantic debates matter little; methodologies, which set the agenda, matter greatly. In respect of the social history of 1660–1832, Englishmen are still burdened with a world-view appropriate to the days when cotton was spun in Manchester, ships built on Clydeside, and coal mined for profit in South Wales.

Keith Hopkins

A recently published papyrus from Roman Egypt, dating from the first or second century AD, contains an appeal by a slave-owner to the authorities for compensation from the careless driver of a donkey, which had run over and seriously injured a young girl on her way to a singing lesson. In her plea, the appellant wrote: 'I loved and cared for this little servant-girl, a house-born slave, in the hope that when she grew up she would look after me in my old age, since I am a helpless women and alone'.

This trivial but fascinating fragment encapsulates many of the problems we face in constructing a social history of the Roman world. First, status fundamentally affected every Roman's life-style and experience. It made a huge difference to be slave or free, rich or poor, young or old, male or female, a solitary widow or the head of a large household. Our consciousness of these status differences should undermine easy generalisations about the Romans as a whole. In this scepticism, I include the generalisations which follow.

Secondly, the whole of Roman society was bedevilled by high mortality, endemic illness and ineffective medicine. The young slave girl, incurably maimed, and the helpless widow were symptoms of a general experience of suffering and violence, against which many Romans defended themselves with a mixture of magic, cruelty and religion. The huge differences between typical modern life experiences and typical Roman experiences of life point up the difficulties of using empathy as a tactic of historical discovery. We cannot easily put ourselves in Roman sandals.

Thirdly, the opening story presents a paradox. The old slave-owner loved her slave; the young slave-girl was taking singing lessons. Both the emotion and the behaviour recorded violate our expectations. Surely that was not how Roman slave-owners normally felt or normally treated their slaves. Probably not. But we should be cautious about imposing our own prejudices and categories on to other societies. That way, we miss half the fun of studying history; that way we look into the past and see only ourselves.

Finally, as with the opening story, most of our evidence about Roman social life is fragmentary. Surviving sources provide only illustrative *vignettes* of daily life. Statistics, which are the bread and butter of modern social and economic history, are missing or, if they do survive, can rarely be trusted. The large gaps in our records highlight the social historian's obligation to reconstruct the past with imagination, even with artistic creativity, but constrained from flights of pure fantasy by the authenticating conventions of scholarship. Imagination is needed, not merely to fill the gaps in our sources, but also to provide the framework, the master picture into which the jigsaw fragments of evidence can be fitted.

Social history is not, or should not be, a blindly accumulated pile of facts (whatever they may be). It should not even be a quilt of testimony, however cunningly devised, each piece cut from abstruse sources. Social history has to be thought out, as well as artfully presented, as a story, a moral tale, a *belle-lettre* or an essay in intellectual adventure. It has to be thought out, because we interpret the past to the present. We cannot confine ourselves to the intentions and perceptions of historical actors. We know what they did not; we know what happened next. We should not throw that advantage away lightly.

We have to identify and to analyse long-term forces, the structures which moulded individual actions, forces of which many actors were often only dimly aware: for example, the growth of Christianity, or the increased costs of defending a large empire against barbarian attacks. And above all, the historian has to choose a topic that interests him and his readers. That is one reason why all history is contemporary history and repeatedly needs to be rewritten. We look into the past and inevitably write something about ourselves.

I began with a triviality – against my better judgement, Trivialities are what social history used to be about: clothes, hunting, sex, weddings, houses, eating, sleeping. For most people, in all periods, major preoccupations; but for serious historians, marginal matters compared with politics, laws, wars and foreign relations. Social history provided mere light relief, the tail-piece for proper history, just enough to convince the reader that the subject matter was human after all.

Fashions have now changed. Social history occupies the centre of the historical stage, thanks to historians like Lawrence Stone, Le Roy Ladurie and Keith Thomas. And, thanks to the work of Norbert Elias, we can see changing habits of eating and love-making, not only as part of the cultural transformation of western civilisation, but also as a reflection of changes in the extent of state power. But that is sociological history, and another story.

David Cannadine

The most famous definition of social history – always quoted, invariably criticised, and never fully understood – is that of G. M. Trevelyan, who began his *English Social History* by defining it as 'the history of the people with the politics left out'. Thus described and practised, social history has been much criticised – for its lack of acquaintance with social theory, for being too concerned with consensus and too little with conflict, for being a series of scenes rather than a serious study of change, for being little more than a nostalgic lament for a vanished world, and for selling so well that it was not merely social history, but a social phenomenon.

Yet, although most social historians today implicitly or explicitly reject Trevelyan's definition, and believe themselves to belong to a more professional, more rigorous, more recent tradition, those who read a little further in his book would be surprised by both the catholicity and contemporaneity of his conception of the subject. To Trevelyan, spelling it out in more detail, social history encompassed the human as well as the economic relations of different classes, the character of family and household life, the conditions of labour and leisure, the attitude of man towards nature, and the cumulative influence of all these subjects on culture, including religion, architecture, literature, music, learning and thought.

This is a formidable and fashionable list. Of course, there was not much sign of such subjects in Trevelyan's own works of synthesis, as the necessary research had not yet been done. And it would be unrealistic and ahistorical to credit him with too much clairvoyance. But in drawing attention to such an agenda of research interests, he certainly anticipated the work of such major scholars of our own day as Eric Hobsbawm, E. P. Thompson, Lawrence Stone, Le Roy Ladurie, Keith Thomas and Peter Laslett. Ironically, the last great practitioner of the old social history was one of the first to foresee the scope and shape of the new.

So Trevelyan might well be pleased with the massive expansion in social history which took place in the three decades since the Second World War and the writing of his most famous book. There is a Social History Society and a *Social History* journal (to say nothing of *Past & Present* and *History Workshop*); almost every reputable publisher seems to have a new social history of England in the course of preparation; many British universities offer social history courses at undergraduate and postgraduate level; and it is a highly popular subject in schools, in extra-mural studies, and on television. In addition, a whole variety of allied subjects – urban history, women's history, family history, the history of crime, of childhood, of education – are its near relatives, each with their own societies, journals and conferences.

But growth can be as disquieting as exhilarating. For as social history becomes more vast and varied, it becomes harder to keep up with it all, and more difficult to define it in any way other than descriptively. Some of its critics (most of whom, incidentally, have never tried their hands at it) condemn it for being no more than an extension of Trevelyan's laundry list, an inchoate amalgam of fashionable fads. Others deride it as a new form of antiquarianism, celebrating 'experience' but eschewing 'explanation'. In reply, its foremost champions (who are not necessarily its foremost practitioners) defend it as an autonomous sub-discipline, intellectually coherent and organisationally confident, offering the best opportunities for the writing of the total history to which, ultimately, we should all aspire.

As with all debates in 'what is history?', most viewpoints are partially valid, few entirely convincing. The real problem with social history, whether done by Trevelyan or anyone else, is that it lacks a hard intellectual centre. Political history is primarily about power, and economic history about money. So, surely, in the same way, social history is about class? Yes, but *what* is class? And *where* is it? There is no theoretical agreement as to its nature; it can barely be said to have existed, even in the western world, before the Industrial Revolution; and too often, social historians spend all their time looking for it, and do not know what to do with it if they find it.

Defining social history is never easy, just as splitting the hairs of Clio's raiment is hard to avoid. In the halcyon days of the 1960s and early 1970s, expansion, proliferation and subdivision were the order of the day, in history as in most other subjects. And of this development, social history was the prime beneficiary. But now retrenchment is upon us; in history as in everything else, amalgamation and rationalisation are in the ascendant; and there are fears that social history, having gained most in the era of expansion, will now suffer most in the age of austerity.

It seems possible, yet unlikely. For social history is surely easier to defend than to define. And in any case, the best social history, whatever it is, is always more than merely that, and its most illustrious practitioners rightly spend more time doing it than defining it. Considering the fate of Trevelyan's misunderstood definition, one can hardly blame them. We would be well advised to follow their example, and get on with it.

FURTHER READING

Abrams, P., *Historical Sociology* (Wells, 1982); Butterfield, H., *The Whig Interpretation of History* (London, 1931); Clark, J. C. D., *English Society 1688–1832: Ideology, Social Structure and Political Practice during the Ancien Régime* (Cambridge, 1985); *Revolution and Rebellion: State and Society in England in the Seventeenth and Eighteenth Centuries* (Cambridge, 1986); 'Eighteenth Century Social History' in

Historical Journal, 27 (1984); Geertz, C., *The Interpretations of Cultures* (New York, 1973); Hobsbawm, E. J., 'From Social History to the History of Society' in *Daedalus* (1971); MacFarlane, A., *The Origins of English Individualism* (Oxford, 1978); McNeill, W. H., *The Pursuit of Power* (Oxford, 1983); Perkin, H., *The Origins of Modern English Society, 1780–1880* (London, 1969); 'Social History', in Finberg, H. P. R. (ed.), *Approaches to History* (London, 1968); Porter, R., *English Society in the Eighteenth Century* (Harmondsworth, 1982); Samuel, R. (ed.), *People's History and Socialist Theory* (London, 1981); Scruton, R., *The Meaning of Conservatism* (Harmondsworth, 1980); Spence, J. D., *Emperor of China* (Harmondsworth, 1977); Thomas, K., *Religion and the Decline of Magic* (London, 1971); *Man and the Natural World: Changing Attitudes in England 1500–1800* (London, 1983); Thompson, E. P., *The Making of the English Working Class* (Harmondsworth edition, 1968); Tosh, J., *The Pursuit of History: Aims, Methods and New Directions in the Study of Modern History* (Harlow, 1984); Trevelyan, G. M., *English Social History* (one volume edition with an introduction by Asa Briggs, Harlow, 1983); Veyne, P., *Writing History* (Middleton, Conn., 1984).

THE CONTRIBUTORS

John Breuilly is Lecturer in History at the University of Manchester, and the author of *Nationalism and the State* (Manchester, 1982).

David Cannadine is Fellow of Christ's College, Cambridge, and editor of *Politicians, Power and Politics in Nineteenth-Century Towns* (Leicester, 1982).

J. C. D. Clark is Fellow of All Souls, Oxford, and the author of *English Society, 1688–1832* (Cambridge, 1985).

Keith Hopkins is Professor of Ancient History at the University of Cambridge and author of *Death and Renewal*, (Cambridge, 1985).

Raphael Samuel is Tutor at Ruskin College, Oxford, and on the editorial collective of *History Workshop Journal*.

5 WHAT IS
RELIGIOUS HISTORY . . . ?

*The history of ecclesiastical structures? The link between
denominations and social change? The history of Christian
doctrine? The study of formal beliefs? What people believed?
What is religious history?*

Patrick Collinson

'Religious history' was not, until recently, an expression much
used, and it has not been as fully institutionalised, academically
and pedagogically, as 'Ecclesiastical History', which for generations
was an examinable subject for ordinands and other students of
Theology. A subject known as 'The History of Religions' turns out,
upon examination, to resemble what used to be called 'Comparative
Religion', not particularly historical at all. So we may begin by
defining Ecclesiastical History. This is clearly the parent discipline.
The editor of a recent volume of essays called *Religion and the People
800–1700* (James Obelkevich) was making, as it were, an adolescent
and generational protest when he announced: 'the authors have
broken with the related discipline of ecclesiastical history and have
abandoned its confines and conventions'.

Eusebius of Caesarea wrote a book called *Ecclesiastical History* in
the fourth century AD. This work both observed and entrenched
certain conventions but by the historiographical standards of
antiquity it was not at all confining. Eusebius was almost the first
historian in the classical tradition to expand the scope of his enquiry
to embrace the experience of ordinary folk, the *laos* or people of
God, many of them martyrs for the faith. Eusebius also respected
documents and made ample use of them. Similarly, sixteenth-
century ecclesiastical historians writing in the age of the Reformation in the Eusebian tradition, like the English martyrologist John
Foxe, were progressive (if we are allowed to write in such Whiggish
terms) in the breadth of their social sympathy and their fidelity to
the documentary record.

Yet it would be absurd to pretend that the confessional and
institutional commitments of most ecclesiastical historians were
anything but a liability. In the centuries of bitterly divided loyalties,
rival confessions gave birth to distorted, false histories. And
devotion to ecclesiastical bodies and institutions expressed by

clerical historians led to an excessively institutional history, full of nothing but hierarchies, liturgies and other forms and structures. In the nineteenth century Carlyle complained of an ecclesiastical history which turned upon 'the outward mechanism, the mere hulks and superficial accidents of the object, . . . as if the Church lay in Bishops' Chapter Houses and Ecumenical Council Halls and Cardinals' Conclaves and not far more in the hearts of believing men'. A full hundred years later, a teacher of the subject in a Nottingham seminary confessed: 'The very name of Church History is often associated with sheer boredom'.

Nevertheless, bishops and councils deserve to be studied and, in this country, both the Ecclesiastical History Society and the *Journal of Ecclesiastical History* are strongly supported institutions. There are university history departments which contain more ecclesiastical specialists than students of secular politics, if only for the arbitrary reason that ecclesiastical archives, until recently little known or exploited, have yielded attractive and rewarding research topics. But many and perhaps most of these specialists now declare an interest in 'popular religion'. With Christopher Hill, they want to know not what 'most people' were *supposed* to believe but what they in fact believed, and what is more, what their belief meant to them; its function. The range of belief now acknowledged to have mattered in people's lives has been greatly extended in the historian's perception, as, for example, in Keith Thomas's *Religion and the Decline of Magic*. Obscure and Byzantine though 'cardinals's conclaves' no doubt are, this is a much more demanding study than traditional ecclesiastical history. It moves beyond observing one's fellow passengers in a railway carriage to trying to converse with them and even to read their inmost thoughts.

But what *is* religion? It is a question which historians have scarcely bothered to ask, although anthropologists have debated it inconclusively for a hundred years. Is it belief in divine beings and all that accompanies such a belief, or a kind of ultimate concern, the groundwork of social existence? And if the latter, where do we draw the line? Is all human experience and therefore all history religious? There is some danger that the coming generations of historians, having little direct experience of religion in the conventional sense, will be too ready to collapse it into something else: most probably social protest or its converse, 'social control'. Others, reacting, may fall into the errors parodied by the poet Browning in *Bishop Blougram's Apology*:

> You'll say, once all believed, man, woman, child,
> In that dear middle-age these noodles praise.

But what *did* they believe?

Christopher Brooke

A wider and a deeper interest in other faiths and in comparative religion is one of the happiest developments of modern scholarship, but my own studies have their centre in the Christian Church. A Christian who meditates deeply on his faith must be concerned with history in some sense and some degree; for Christianity is an historical religion, inescapably tied to the events of Jesus' life – not to particular interpretations of particular moments in it, nor to a particular theological interpretation of the Incarnation or the Atonement – but, as I once heard a schoolmaster put it to his class, when speaking of the events of Christmas, reverently, but firmly, 'no baby, no Church'. This means that the Christian faith is a constant inspiration to an historian; but it does not mean that believing Christians have any necessary advantage in the study of religious history, nor of Christian origins. They are more likely perhaps to be interested; but it is fundamental to the modern study of religious history that it has been fruitfully pursued by people of every faith and none.

There are no watertight compartments in the study of the past. Religious history is not an entity, utterly distinct from secular or social or political or economic or intellectual history. The religious historian will do an inferior job if he has not at least an inkling of many other specialisms. As historians, we live in a large and ample room – in which we meet people of every race and colour and religious and political creed. It seems to me quite natural, for example, that the study of the history of the Church was one of the most creative sciences in the scientific revolution of the seventeenth century. In the nineteenth century another approach to history, equally ideological though in a very different way, made the writings of Karl Marx immensely fruitful and influential in stimulating new historical currents. Serious advance in historical science in the seventeenth century involved the application of scepticism – commonly by deeply religious, fervent Christians – to current credulity and superstition. But this was not incompatible with a dogmatic faith, though dogma and historical enquiry can be as easily enemies as friends, as many found in the era of Darwin and the biblical critics of the nineteenth century. Yet the same nineteenth century saw a new system, fully as dogmatic as the old, rise out of the historical speculations of Marx – and those of us who are not wedded to the dogma are liable to think his system often in conflict with the historical enquiries which (like the seventeenth-century Church) Marxism has so enormously stimulated.

This illustrates the fundamental point. If the historian of religion tries to divorce himself or herself wholly from his belief, he deceives himself and his hearers, and is liable to be convicted of cynicism or blindness. Yet if he is wholly possessed by his beliefs, and cannot talk the same language as those who believe them not – if he cannot work in the same room with the people who used to be called heretics and unbelievers – he is not engaged in a serious, academic or scientific enquiry at all. This is one of the greatest challenges a modern academic has to face – and most of us face it most of the time so successfully that our students think us cynics, and judge our disciplines to be irrelevant.

I am myself a medievalist and have spent much time in recent years studying the history of marriage. Here is an institution which goes right to the heart of the problem of religious history. It was and is a Christian sacrament; it is the centre of all that is fashionable in social history today; much of the political history of the Middle Ages turned on dynastic schemes and marriages. Some of its problems, as one meets them in the Middle Ages, seem strangely remote. 'Till death us do part' in the Middle Ages meant – for most people – about ten years, or twenty if they were lucky, or, as it might be, very unlucky. Divorce in the modern sense was forbidden by the Church's laws. There were all sorts of escape routes; yet many people for much of the time did not think of following them.

It has been fashionable among some modern social historians to claim that modern attitudes to married love and domestic intimacy were invented in some later century – they differ as to which. This is not so. There are great difficulties in penetrating to the heart of marriage, and of its status in the face of other human relationships. But it is quite clear that every variety of attitude and approach was possible in the Middle Ages. Men and women married for money and aggrandisement and security and comfort, and out of gratitude and love. We can even catch some glimpses of the way in which these very different attitudes were brought together in the liturgy and theology of the sacrament. One central piece of evidence lies in the letters which the distinguished Abbess Heloïse wrote to Abelard, now for long years a monk, about their former life of love and marriage. For here we see two of the most acute theological minds of the twelfth century searching for a reconciliation between the deepest of human experiences, carnal and spiritual, in a sacrament which is performed by the partners. The range of problems they faced illustrates how relevant – how desperately relevant – such studies can be to the predicaments of the modern world, fascinated by the lofty claims of marriage, yet contemplating its unequal struggle against many other relationships; and how the religious historian must be something of a virtuoso, now in the most abstract realms of spiritual experience and theological speculation, and the next minute among the most earthly and earthy of human events and experiences.

Edward Norman

The very words 'ecclesiastical history' now sound rather antique, and it is true that the subject they describe has been broadened and transformed enormously in recent decades. As traditionally practised, from Bede to the denominational chronicles still being written, church history was moralistic and didactic: it was intended to demonstrate religious truth by disclosing the divine guidance supposedly evident in the development of the institutions of Christianity. Thus Southey, in his *Book of the Church* (1824), declared that his intention was to dispel 'heathenish delusions' and 'the errors and crimes of the Romish Church', and to illustrate 'the day-break of the Reformation'. Church history also tended to be rather narrowly national, and even F. D. Maurice, who had real insights into the fallibility of human institutions, felt able to assert, in 1838, that 'England has been the centre of all religious movements that have occurred'.

Yet even more than most other branches of history, the historical study of religion has been reconstructed with materials provided by the social sciences; for some of the most seminal sociological theory; like that of Weber and Troeltsch, derived from studies of religious phenomena. Just as in the nineteenth century it was historical relativism rather than scientific discovery that induced intellectual doubts about religious claims (it was the realisation that the evidences and structures of Christianity and its Jewish foundations were very like other religious systems found in widely varying societies), so in the twentieth century it has been the analysis of the non-religious reasons for which people hold to religious practice and belief that has dissolved away the priority of 'ecclesiastical' over 'religious' history. The major advances in the subject are now those which relate the history of the churches to 'secular' developments.

Denominational histories are still being produced – and they are still of great value. But contemporary emphasis is upon the ways in which each individual denomination responds to external influences: to the social changes of the times, to economic conditions, to the impact of intellectual orthodoxies, and so forth. The other great emphasis is upon the life of the grass-roots. This, too, is hugely necessary; but there is a risk of exclusivity in those whose enthusiasm to learn about the practices of the ordinary church member in the provincial chapel produces impatience with the study of church leaders and theologians. A balance is needed, and the application of the same canons in religious history as obtain in other areas of history. There is a legitimate – even necessary – division of labour: few would expect a study of, for example, the fiscal policies of Sir Robert Peel to dwell extensively upon the economic perceptions of the electorate of, say, Newcastle. It is for others, specialists in social and economic history, to write of Newcastle opinion. Similarly, in religious history, there has to be comparable sophistication. Not every study of 'the Church' in a given period has to embrace – as 'secular' histories in general do not embrace – both central and local phenomena. It is a careful and balanced recognition of the inter-relationship of the two which will make for authentic professionalism, and for the most valuable advances in the subject. But specialisation has to persist.

In view of the modern emphasis on the secular influences in the development of religious institutions it is surprising that 'secular' historians do not take religious history more seriously: For it has to be observed that the contemporary secular intellectual, unable to experience the importance of religion for himself, is unable to appreciate its importance for others. This can often lead to a serious distortion of the motives and preoccupations of the men and women of the past. Anyone concerned with the teaching of history, in schools and universities, will know how difficult it is to persuade pupils that religious belief was a crucial and often determining consideration in the formation of past culture. The absence of a contemporary secular alternative in the place traditionally filled by religious observance – and the consequent intellectual disorientation means that there is not even a modern substitute from whose dimensions and sacral qualities modern pupils can grasp the shape of the past. Historians of religion have only themselves to blame if they cannot write with those graphic qualities required to give an impression of the importance of their subject. 'Profane historians', Acton said in 1859, 'have yet a lesson to learn from the method of ecclesiastical history'.

Peter Lake

The definitions game is always more fun for the spectator than the participants. I am no more capable of defining religion than I am of defining history. What follows will be no more than a set of circumlocutionary exercises designed to explain the sort of assumptions and aspirations with which one 'working historian' of one section of the Christian tradition approaches his material laced, I fear, with some baldly prescriptive statements about what 'religious history' should be like. The subject matter of the religious historian I take to be any set of actions or beliefs which either their author or other contemporaries subjected to a religious interpretation. By a religious interpretation I mean any reading which involved either the honour and worship of God or the attainment of salvation by men.

In playing definitions it is usual to go on about how one's subject really is part of a seamless web and in fact contains virtually every other sort of history imaginable. Such an option is certainly open to the historian of early modern Christianity. A whole series of attempts have been made to 'read off' contemporary social and political attitudes from ostensibly religious statements and actions, on the assumption that once religion is regarded as the idiom through which contemporaries conducted their arguments about such subjects, the process whereby the historian can decide whether what they 'really' meant provides no difficulty. It is not necessary to go to the opposite extreme and claim, with Professor Bossy, that since contemporaries viewed society in religious terms and were unable to conceive of the dichotomy between 'religion' and 'society' all such projects represent fundamental lapses from historical propriety. I would argue, however, that religious history can only retain a certain coherence and integrity if its practitioners insist that their range of interest is limited to those areas of experience and action which contemporaries subjected to religious interpretation. That said, it remains the case that the resulting area of legitimate interest is large enough to satisfy the appetites of the greediest historiographical imperialist. Since many contemporaries invested the course of international politics with eschatological significance the religious historian can well claim a legitimate interest if not in Elizabethan foreign policy *tout court*, then, at least, in the ideological co-ordinates within which much of that policy was formulated.

More important than a licence to steal other historians' subjects, however, such a view means that religious history must, in the broadest sense, be regarded as a branch of intellectual history – or rather of the history of human consciousness. It must relate to the meanings and interpretations with which historical agents invested their own actions and lives. This is to accept the now well-known dichotomy between religious and ecclesiastical history. Of course, very often the religious historian uses the formal records of the church and is, therefore, duty bound to analyse the structure of the institutions which produced those records. However, the study of those institutions remains a branch of administrative rather than of religious history and the tendency whereby religious history is transmuted into the study of the institutions of the church needs to be resisted. Religious history is not the history of the church, defined as a bureaucratic structure of jurisdictional unit, rather it is the history of the religious sentiments or values to which the church's employees (the clergy) and its clients (the laity) subscribed.

In describing religious history as to do with meaning, it is important not to accept what might be called a 'Protestant' fallacy which tends to identify the study of meaning with the study of formal belief. It is important to remember that if religious history should not be collapsed into ecclesiastical history, on the one hand, it should not be collapsed into the history of Christian doctrine, on the other. A knowledge of and interest in formal doctrine is a *sine qua non* for any religious historian but his or her concerns should encompass the search for implicit meanings in religious practice and observance as well as for formal meanings explicit in theological argument. In that search caution needs to be exercised lest too incoherent and inchoate an animism be imputed to the inarticulate masses of early modern Europe. Too rigid and mechanical a functionalism in the analysis of 'magical' or 'superstitious' beliefs has marred some pioneering attempts to explicate the religious component in early modern 'popular culture', although given the very difficult nature of the sources it is far easier to carp about such failures in theory than to avoid them in practice.

If religious history is part of the history of human consciousness, is it in fact a part, even a major part, of the history of false consciousness? When ecclesiastical history was the preserve of the ordained and the pious such questions hardly arose. Now that secularisation has caught up with the history of the Christian tradition itself it occurs with rather greater force. How far are people located outside that tradition able to comment sympathetically on its history? It is certainly true that a theological training of the sort to which few non-Christians can aspire is a great help to the religious historian. Conversely, it could be argued that an indifference to contemporary theological issues enables the historian to approach the religious values and disputes of the past with some sort of open mind. In practice it seems to me that a practical agnosticism represents an acceptable (if not the best) response to these difficulties. Certainly, religious history must retain *religion* as the centre of its concern; too radical an atheism, too stringent a drive to 'read' religious impulses and experiences as really something else – the product of political, social or sexual divisions, conflicts or solidarities – not only destroys the integrity of the subject, it fundamentally subverts the authenticity of that reconstruction of the experience, choices and cognitive structures of particular groups or individuals which I take it to be the religious historians' job to produce.

David Hempton

In the past twenty years religious history has widened its scope to take into account the full range of social, economic, cultural and political life within which religion must be located. Since history is not a separate compartment in the intellectual mansion, and since religion has impinged on all aspects of human life in one form or another, the religious historian needs to be familiar with a wide range of disciplines from theology to sociology. Indeed, any light from whatever source is valuable, so long as it is genuinely illuminating and not, as has sometimes been the case, merely dazzling. Much illumination has come recently from those concerned more with the religion of the people than with ecclesiastical or theological élites. The great acreage of ignorance about religion at a popular level has now been reduced, though there is still much to be done. Moreover, this is difficult land to cultivate despite the new implements of statistical analysis, anthropological techniques, and the more skilful investigation of popular culture. More knowledge, especially of local history, has inevitably resulted in greater complexity.

Recent work on the history of Methodism, for example, has drawn attention to its remarkable expansion in the British Isles in the decades after 1790. The range of explanations offered by historians illustrate new dimensions to the social history of religion. Methodist growth has been interpreted as both a component of the psychic process of counter-revolution and as a religious expression of popular radicalism. Its success has been attributed to weaknesses in Anglican parochial machinery and to its creative interaction with English popular culture through shared superstitions. Its growth has been related to specific kinds of community, to certain occupational groups, and to the booms and slumps of the economy. Some argue that Methodist revivalism had an internal dynamic of its own, and was based more on religious zeal than on social determinants. More traditional Methodist historians still like to emphasise Methodism's Arminian theology, pragmatic organisation, standards of pastoral care, innovations in worship and community solidarity. Still others have tried to shed light on Methodist expansion by comparing it with similar developments in continental Europe and America.

Such explanations are not, of course, mutually exclusive and there is some material to support all of them; but establishing priorities with limited evidence is not easy. Even when the 'why' question is satisfactorily answered, other problems remain. Within Methodism what were the respective roles of clergy and laity, rich and poor, men and women, and parents and children? How did Methodists relate to other denominations and to their surrounding culture? How did religion affect their ethical standards, their social and economic relationships, and their political consciousness? To what extent, and in what form, do complex theological ideas filter

down into popular perceptions? In short, how religious are supposedly religious people and how irreligious is the rest of the
population? Such questions ought to make it clear that the social
historian of religion is operating in rather different territory from
historical theologians and denominational reconstructionists; but
the links between them must be preserved to save religious history
from an undue concentration on theologians and denominations,
and from those who would see religion as a mere product of social
forces. Ultimately, the best religious history is written by those who
combine a deep insight into the nature of religious forms and
experiences with a proper understanding of their social setting.

FURTHER READING

Bossy, J., *Christianity in the West* (Oxford, 1985); Brooke, Chris-
topher, *Medieval Church and Society* (London, 1971); *Marriage in
Christian History* (Cambridge, 1978); Butterfield, H., *Christianity and
History* (London, 1949); Chadwick, O., *Catholicism and History*
(Cambridge, 1978); Collinson, P., *Godly People* (London, 1983); (ed.),
Beginning Church History (London, forthcoming); Coolidge, J. S.,
Puritanism and the Bible (Oxford, 1970); Dodd, C. H., *The Parables of
the Kingdom* (London, 1935); *The Apostolic Preaching and its Develop-
ments* (London, 1936); *The Founder of Christianity* (New York and
London, 1970–1); Gilbert, A. D., *Religion and Society in Industrial
England: Church, Chapel and Social Change, 1740–1914* (Harlow,
1976); Greyerz, K. von, *Religion and Society in Early Modern Europe,
1500–1800* (London, 1984); Hill, M., *A Sociology of Religion* (London,
1973); Knowles, D., *Great Historical Enterprises* (1982); Laqueur,
T. W., *Religion and Respectability: Sunday Schools and Working-Class
Culture, 1780–1850* (New Haven, 1976); Obelkevich, J., *Religion and
Rural Society: South Lindsey, 1825–1875* (Oxford, 1976); (ed.),
Religion and the People, 800–1700 (Carolina, 1979); Sharpe, E. J.,
Understanding Religion (London, 1983); Sykes, N., *Man as Church-
man* (Cambridge, 1960); Thomas, K., *Religion and the Decline of
Magic* (London, 1971); Valenze, D. M., *Prophetic Sons and Daugh-
ters: Female Preaching and Popular Religion in Industrial England*
(Princeton, 1985); Ward, W. R., *Religion and Society in England,
1790–1850* (London, 1972).

THE CONTRIBUTORS

Christopher Brooke is Dixie Professor of Ecclesiastical History at the University of Cambridge and co-author of *Popular Religion in the Middle Ages, 1000–1300* (London, 1983).

Patrick Collinson is Professor of Modern History at the University of Sheffield and author of *The Religion of Protestants: the Church in English Society, 1559–1625* (Oxford, 1984).

David Hempton is Lecturer in Modern History at The Queen's University, Belfast, and author of *Methodism and Politics in British Society, 1750–1850* (London, 1984).

Peter Lake is Lecturer in English History at Royal Holloway and Bedford New College, University of London, and author of *Moderate Puritans and the Elizabethan Church* (Cambridge, 1982).

Edward Norman is the Dean of Peterhouse, Cambridge, and author of *The English Church in the Nineteenth Century* (Oxford, 1984).

6. WHAT IS
THE HISTORY OF
SCIENCE . . . ?

*A cultural ornament to science? An insignificant sub-
speciality within history? Plotting the progress of scientific
discovery towards truth? A social activity, a form of culture
like any other? The study of man's changing understanding
of the world of nature? What is the history of science?*

Roy Porter

A great transformation is under way in how we view the history of
science.

When, at the turn of this century, J. B. Bury proclaimed, 'history is
a science, no less and no more', he was giving science his vote of
confidence. Bury's confidence was widespread. For Victorian minds
like his, science was an engine in the intellectual world no less
mighty than the steam engine in the industrial. Honest doubters of
course voiced their fears (was not science eroding faith and killing
poetry?), but science's success in unveiling Nature's laws and
transforming material life seemed beyond cavil. As Macaulay sang
the praises of Baconian science:

> It has lengthened life, it has mitigated pain, it has extinguished
> diseases, . . . these are but a part of its fruits and of its first
> fruits. For it is a philosophy which never rests, which has
> never attained, which is never perfect. Its law is progress.

Thus to our grandfathers, science was the epitome both of objectivity and utility. It was right that primitive thought-forms like
magic were crumbling before science's hard facts and conclusive
experiments; good that the humanities themselves were becoming
scientific (as Bury thought was happening to history). Not surprisingly then the aim of traditional history of science was clear-cut. It
was to trace the march of mind, to show, for instance, how in
astronomy Ptolemy had yielded to Copernicus, how in physics
Newton had superseded Descartes. For, ultimately, Ptolemy and
Descartes had been wrong, Copernicus and Newton right.

This conception of writing the history of science by plotting its
progress towards truth has continued to be influential this century,

and it has been reinforced by growing acknowledgement of the role played by science in making Western civilisation unique. Thus, as Herbert Butterfield put it, the Scientific Revolution from Copernicus to Newton wrought such changes as to put both the Renaissance and the Reformation in the shade. It remains the creed of popularisers such as Carl Sagan and Isaac Asimov, and is central to Daniel Boorstin's new survey of *The Discoverers*.

Yet it is being overturned. Revisionist historians of science have reminded us how general history freed itself long ago from religious or political bias, concluding that judging the past by the present produces bad history. But aren't we making the same mistake if we tell the history of science, using hindsight, from the viewpoint of today's astronomy or physics? Too often this approach ('Whig history') paints a canvas depicting, on the one hand, heroic precursors, passing down the baton of truth in the relay race of discovery; and, on the other hand, knaves and fools (such as anti-evolutionists) who got it all wrong. In such Manichee history, the errors of the also-rans get attributed to their psychology and prejudices (e.g. religious dogma), whereas, by contrast, the triumphs of the winners are explained by genius. Theirs are the minds which soar into the stratosphere of intellect, thinking higher, purer thoughts.

But we must reject these 'saints and sinners' caricatures. We shouldn't take sides. Losers need study as much as winners. For example, don't neglect Descartes (as Asimov does) merely because it was the Newtonian not the Cartesian laws of mechanics that ultimately triumphed. For Descartes was a key figure in his own day and immensely influential.

Furthermore, the historian mustn't just stand back and admire genius; he must anatomise the thought-worlds of the 'discoverers'. It begs too many questions to see Newton as 'discovering' the law of gravity merely by dint of the exercise of his towering rationality. Indeed, put his mind under the microscope, and does he even look so rational? For Newton was deeply absorbed in alchemy, in Neo-Platonic philosophy, and in millennialist theology. Nor were these mere hobbies; more likely they were integral to his scientific achievements. Alchemy's doctrine of sympathies probably attuned Newton to the notion of attraction, so vital to universal gravitation; while Neo-Platonism's quest for the immaterial probably persuaded him that the universe was almost entirely pure space, a void. So the inspirations of science turn out to be varied and complex, and include outlooks we'd nowadays see as unscientific.

Above all, the new history of science is on its guard against interpreting science's past by present scientific orthodoxy. Take the history of evolutionism. For the last half century the Darwinian theory (evolution works chiefly through natural selection) has been in the driving-seat. So historians have heaped their attentions on Darwin, to the neglect of other evolutionists such as Lamarck. And there have been strenuous efforts to prove that Darwin 'discovered' natural selection 'scientifically', rather than through extraneous stimuli, e.g. after reading Malthus' account of the struggle for survival. But right now biologists are again having grave doubts about the part played by natural selection, stressing instead the role of random variation. Must we therefore start rewriting our histories? That would turn history into a service industry for science itself, which would be akin to intellectual treason.

We live in paradoxical times. Science flourishes as never before. But we are becoming less sure whether it is a blessing or a bane. And, not least, following Einstein and Heisenberg, even the very notion of scientific truth is in the melting pot. In this situation, the job of the historian of science is not to play historiographer royal to science, but to undertake detached analysis of how science really operates, and to examine its place within the wider spheres of thought, culture and society.

Steven Shapin

Amongst historical specialities, the history of science has a unique problem. Is it history at all? We take history to be the record of human affairs and actions. Yet the received view of science is that it is founded upon entities which are not man-made: science is based not upon artefacts but upon facts. Scientific matters of fact, along with certain privileged ways of accounting for them (laws, theories) are widely held to be discovered rather than invented. In this received view, we can record the history of discoverers, but that which they discover (objective scientific knowledge) must lie without the scope of historical inquiry.

It follows from the received view that science, considered as the corpus of objective knowledge and as an activity governed by a special method, is not a typical form of culture or a typical human pursuit. Thus the history of science is fundamentally different from the history of art, religion, philosophy or politics. Perhaps the history of scientific errors, delusions and by-ways belongs to history proper, but not the history of *science*.

Over the past fifteen or twenty years, this received view of science and its historical study has been systematically challenged. It is now widely, if not universally, maintained that science is a social activity and a form of culture like any other, and that it may be studied and understood accordingly. The challenge has come from three main sources: from the discipline called the history of science and the consequent loosening of its ties to the scientific community as a constituency for its products; from the development of a significant anti-realist and anti-rationalist strand in the philosophy of science; and, perhaps most importantly, from the growth (especially in Britain and on the Continent) of a serious sociology of scientific knowledge, and from increasing contacts between sociologists and historians equally concerned to understand the realities of scientific practice.

Understanding science as a social activity and as a typical form of culture means that we treat it as goal-directed: we move beyond asking what scientists believe to asking what they are trying to do; it means that we understand beliefs in terms of the inherited and socially-transmitted stock of knowledge available to scientists in their particular settings and in terms of their purposes; it entails understanding the meaning of scientific propositions by referring to their context of use; and it allows us to seek to *explain* scientists' beliefs, whether 'true' or 'false', using the full range of resources available to the historian.

The history of science is a predominantly empirical discipline, and its practitioners have engaged with these projects at a concrete and particular level, generally neglecting the abstract and programmatic arguments of philosophical and sociological theorists. Nevertheless, the body of empirical work which implicitly rejects the received view of science and its history is already impressively large; and existing empirical work has precipitated research programmes of its own. For example, historians have recently shown that in the seventeenth century scientific propositions (including Boyle's and Newton's) were evaluated not only according to their adequacy in technical contexts of use but also according to their value in justifying particular conceptions of God's attributes and the correct moral order of society. Nature was available for such usages because it was conceived to be divine, a theatre for God's activity, a reservoir of moral meaning that might be drawn upon as required to comment upon human conduct.

Suppose it were objected that only past science, pre-professionalised science, can be understood as a typical form of culture. Once, by the end of the nineteenth century, science became properly professionalised, it ceased to be a part of society and a part of the general culture. It would follow that at that moment science ceases to be amenable to truly historical inquiry. The point is an important one for the academic study of science: the sorts of 'social influences' upon science which historians have documented in the seventeenth and eighteenth centuries become much more difficult to trace in the science of modern times. Here is a potential programme for historical research: what were the connections between the professionalisation and differentiation of scientific culture and the development of secular views of nature?

As it happens, modern physical science has been one of the most vigorously worked seams of recent social studies of science. This is where the history of science and the micro-sociology of scientific knowledge approach each other so closely as to be indistinguishable. The goals of present-day high-energy physicists may no longer include comment upon the order of the wider society, but modern science is no less goal-directed, no less socially transmitted, and scientific statements are no less dependent for their meaning upon the context of practical activity.

The programme for the history of science is, therefore, to be *history* everywhere in its domain. This programme entails understanding scientific knowledge as the product of human activity. To paraphrase Marx on history:

> Nature does nothing . . . It is rather man, real living man who does everything.

Simon Schaffer

One of the earliest attempts to define the scope of the history of science – and, at the same time, to recommend it to a wide popular readership – was that of the radical Dissenter and heroic chemist Joseph Priestley. By 1767, he had completed a lengthy survey of discoveries in the science of electricity made since the earliest times. While his book aimed to cover the whole history of this science, more than one half of the book was needed to deal with the mass of work done in electricity in just the past twenty years. This striking demonstration of cumulative and accelerating progress was Priestley's main concern. It has been the main concern of historians of science ever since. The doyens of twentieth-century history of science, such as George Sarton in the 1930s, made this kind of history the noblest and the most virtuous work any chronicler could perform, just because this was the only activity which the human race had developed which was always progressive, always successful, and increasingly revealing of truth. Priestley put it bluntly: 'civil history', the story of politics and statecraft, 'presents nothing but a tedious uniformity', and any sensitive reader could not 'help being shocked with a view of the vices and miseries of mankind'. By contrast, science itself while virtuous, could not engage our interest because it lacked the human angle. Thus history of science was the best of all forms of history, since it was 'relieved from what is most tedious and disgusting' and at the same time presented 'the human understanding grasping at the noblest objects'. This sales pitch made history of science the best reading matter for an enlightened market.

But in the 1960s something started to go very wrong with this splendid vision. History of science has increasingly turned dirty. 'The vices and miseries of mankind' are now more visible in the stories historians tell about science than almost anywhere else. We were told that Isaac Newton was an autocrat, deeply disturbed by radical critics, Roman Catholicism, and continental operators. Louis Pasteur, cynosure of pure experimenters, suppressed his data, organised campaigns of slander against scientific rivals, and engineered wholescale coups in the polity of nineteenth-century France. More recently, even apparently 'hard' areas of scientific knowledge, such as mathematical statistics, quantum theory, or observational geology, have proved accessible to ingenious historians who have displayed the social interests which sustained claims to truth, and have analysed the cultural wiles which scientists use to make their views stick. Simultaneously, areas of knowledge hitherto quite outside the accepted boundaries of real science, such as phrenology, astrology or mesmerism, have been treated in just the same way as historians treat our own favoured forms of truth. In the conditions of the seventeenth century, the contest between the Society of Astrologers and the critics of judicial astrology is not to be understood as the obvious and inevitable triumph of reason over obscurantism. Historians have become so suspicious of this obviousness that they have begun to avoid using it as an explanatory principle.

The loss of the obvious is probably the most striking aspect of this change in historiography. In Priestley's time, European culture encountered fresh evidence of the enormous cultural diversity of human experience, whether in the South Seas or in the streets of Paris. It is as though this clash has at last reached the final haven of western European culture – natural science itself. For the principal resources on which the historians of science rely are those developed in the fields of cultural anthropology and comparative sociology. Just as in New Guinea a cassowary is, for some people, not a bird at all, so, in Wiltshire in 1774, the air generated when calcined lead was heated was just not oxygen. It is, of course, quite possible to say that the culture of the New Guinea hill tribes and that of Wiltshire chemists were both mistaken. We know that the cassowary is a bird; we know that calcined lead yields oxygen. But to say as much scarcely allows space for history. This priority has been changed, and the demand is that a space be made where historians can work. It turns out that making that space means getting rid of our obvious assumptions about what is the case in nature. Then historians of science can freely exploit the tools which all other historians have themselves taken for granted. This necessary act of jungle clearance has deep institutional consequences: it brings historians of science closer to other analysts of culture, further from the scientific institutions in which they find themselves. But a more profound understanding of the way science works is a rich reward: it ought to provide science with better means of explaining itself. Priestley agreed:

> These histories are evidently much more necessary in an advanced state of science than in the infancy of it.

Robert M. Young

If science is so important, why is its history so badly served? Most people who read and write history would readily acknowledge that 'science' – broadly conceived as science, technology and medicine – has been crucial in every era and is at the heart of our own. Yet books and articles about the Protestant and Capitalist Revolutions of the seventeenth century manage to be silent about the Scientific Revolution, even though those three fundamental changes were arguably part of a single set of alterations leading to the modern world and world view. Similarly, historians of the Victorian era manage to say little about basic changes of view about 'man's place in nature'.

You can look in vain through many standard histories of these periods for serious coverage of the fundamental alterations in theory and practice which were afoot and which had scientific ideas at their centre. In the seventeenth-century example, the earth was being displaced from the centre of the universe, and our sun was seen as the centre of our system of planets, while the 'perfect' circles travelled by the planets were being replaced by the ellipses. This and other scientific changes, in the study of physics were closely interwoven with developments in theology, mining, ballistics and navigation. Yet they get sequestered into specialist books on the history of science and technology. Why should a new view of our world and how we know it be so isolated?

The Victorian example, is, if anything, even odder. If you look at the contemporary periodicals, magazines and novels which were being read by an increasingly literate public, they are full of the topics which historians of our own day tend to ignore when writing Victorian history. Darwin's theory of evolution by natural selection brought humanity into the world of other animals and fundamentally challenged the special status of 'man' and 'mind'. The writings of the time were full of debates on the concepts which were part of Darwinism, just as Darwinism was part of a wider movement of naturalism and secularisation. Natural laws were applied, for example, to human population growth: Malthus argued that famine, war, pestilence and death were as much the function of scientific laws as the movements of the planets. The history of the earth and of the coming and going of plant and animal species was seen as a natural process, not a result of separate acts of Divine creation and extinction. The mind was increasingly seen as obeying natural laws, based on the functions of the brain, and this challenged traditional ideas of free will and responsibility.

You can find these matters seriously considered in the novels of George Eliot and Benjamin Disraeli and in the Penny Magazines, but not much in our own period's historical works except those specialising in the history of science.

A similar story could be told about most periods, for example, ancient, medieval and Renaissance, Chinese, Arab and American histories. In each case science and other branches of expert knowledge tend to be treated in relative isolation from social, political and other parts of intellectual history. The result is that the academic history of science is in most cases seen as a highly specialised field of esoteric knowledge, while the actual history of science was and is important in social and cultural change.

What forces keep it that way? I would say that our education system is doubly daunting in separating off scientific schooling. Pupils stop doing either science or the arts at an early age and are *taught* to split off scientific knowledge from social, political, economic and cultural knowledge. Arts people end up in awe of science, and scientists end up defensively arrogant about the arts.

In our own time, science, technology and medicine are transforming the conception of babies, education, work, leisure. Think of 'test tube babies', microelectronics, genetic engineering and biotechnology, video, high-technology medicine. If we can't learn to think of science and technology as part of culture in the present, as well as in the past, we will continue to separate them off from debates about social values and goals. We have paid a high price for making this separation, and are in the process of beginning to pay an even higher one. Politics is the setting of priorities – values and goals in action – to shape social policy. This goal-setting determines what priorities are set in science, what research gets done, what theories, therapies and things are available to us. These play a significant role in determining the new technologies that embody the social forces that shape our lives. This was true in the great era of exploration at the end of the Renaissance; it was true in creating manufacture and machinofacture, mass production and automation.

In thinking about this urgent set of issues, I would say that the historian of science should not be an abstruse specialist. She or he belongs in the mainstream of social and cultural debate. If we can't get science integrated into history, we won't see how our own history is being made, and, more importantly, we won't give the public access to how we decide it should be made.

History of science now sits in an uneasy niche as a cultural ornament to science or as a tiny sub-speciality within history. It needs to be treated by historians as the fundamental part of culture that it has always been in practice.

Roger Cooter

The history of science is no longer an isolated discipline inhabited by scientists flattering themselves by ennobling their past. Nor any longer is it a pasture for grazing philosophers treating scientists (or natural philosophers) and their ideas as if they existed in a vacuum, apart from the rest of society. But it would be a mistake to suppose, simply because historical studies of scientific ideas and events now conform better to the norms of scholarship elsewhere in history, that the discipline has become fully a part of history proper. Despite the success of the efforts made since the 1960s to incorporate historical studies of scientific activity into the rest of history, the history of science as a discipline remains separate (presumably, therefore, for reasons other than the body of material upon which it focuses). Arguably, it is the very success of the efforts made since the 1960s that, paradoxically, has caused the history of science to remain unincorporated. In any event, the present state and outlook of, and regard for, the history of science cannot be defined without referring to its recent past.

For the sake of brevity and convenience, let me confine myself here to one of the interests of my own recent past: the study of those bodies of knowledge that historians previously either dismissed as nonsense or endeavoured to exploit for the purpose of benchmarking the progress of scientific truth. As I argued in 1976 (*History of Science*), the coming together of scholars on such issues as alchemy, astrology, mesmerism, phrenology and spiritualism was not a sign of growing antiquarianism, but rather a manifestation of current concern over the location and, in some cases, the existence of legitimate boundaries between science, 'pseudoscience', and society. The examination of the controversies over such practices and bodies of knowledge made it apparent that only with hindsight could one sharply distinguish between science and objective facticity, on the one hand, and 'pseudoscience', 'scientism', ideology and social values and interests on the other. Just as the theoretical elaboration and deployment of some of the so-called pseudo-sciences could be shown to be inseparable from their producers' and deployers' social interests, so the knowledge and methodologies that established themselves as 'scientific' could likewise be shown to be social and ideological. The point made was that science and the distinction between it and non-science was not universal, neutral and eternal as positivist philosophers and historians had implied; what was deemed 'natural' or 'scientific knowledge' and the process by which it was distinguished from 'the social' and 'the cultural' was historically determined, or was the outcome of particular social interests negotiated in particular social contexts.

Quite aside from the fact that studies such as those on rejected scientific knowledge were fundamentally committed to the principal object of history – to explain and account for change – they had a profound implication for a history of science regarded as separate from the rest of history. Because science was shown by its very nature to be social and ideological (in addition to whatever else it is), the history of science could not be rendered other than integral to the total history of social relations and structures.

That this conclusion was not welcomed with open arms by all historians of science is hardly surprising. More interesting, though, is how two decades of hard scholarship have been effectively co-opted through the very act of granting legitimacy to 'social history' of science. Thus labelled and cast (wittingly or unwittingly) merely as the study of science *in relation to external social 'factors'*, the historical studies that had revealed science as integral to the history of society as a whole were opened to marginalisation, whenever and wherever expedient. Moreover, through the same act of acknowledgement, a pardon was given to historical studies of science that were entirely within the history and philosophy of thought.

Thus the history of science today is far from uniform in its historiographical outlook. Instead of having become fully a part of history, the discipline often appears hardly less separate than before. Indeed, it seems in some danger of regressing into isolation as a result of failing to understand and/or to heed its own historical counsel.

Maurice Crosland

Much of history has understandably been focused on mankind, with little attention being paid to his natural environment. The history of science is related equally to humanity and the natural world. We might consider the history of science as a study of man's changing understanding of the world of nature. Some people, on seeing the word 'science' assume something modern and very technical, probably associated with a laboratory. But science began with a commonsense interpretation of the world around us, which later became more sophisticated and only in the last century became separated from other studies by specialisation.

The ancient and medieval worlds in which man, the microcosm, was influenced by the macrocosm, the old world of harmony, purpose and design was to be transformed in early modern Europe by new ideas in natural philosophy. The natural world continued, however, to provide a model for human society as, for example, in the organisation of the state. In the seventeenth century the institution of the monarchy was upheld both on the analogy of the position of the sun in the 'universe' (solar system) in the heliocentric theory of Copernicus and by analogy with the heart in the body in the physiology of William Harvey. In the eighteenth century interpretations of nature provided a model for a new approach to law, religion and society. In the nineteenth century Darwin's theory of natural selection was seized upon as justification for two extreme but opposite political viewpoints. There can be no doubt about the power of scientific ideas.

There are many different approaches to the history of science but an encouraging feature over the past decade has been the replacement of much of the old 'internalist' (or science-centred) history of science by a broader contextual approach which relates science to the society of the day. One valuable genre in the history of science is the biographical approach, since the researcher is forced to look at the subject's life and surroundings as well as his work.

A few years ago I chose to study the French scientist, Gay-Lussac, as a prominent example of one of the first generation of professional scientists which emerged in the eventful period immediately after the French revolution, a revolution which had a major influence on the organisation of science and medicine as well as on the social order. Moreover, Gay-Lussac not only became one of France's leading scientists in the early nineteenth century, he also applied science for commercial and industrial purposes and was elected a member of the Chamber of Deputies. The resulting book is therefore a case study of the interaction of science and society in a specific historical context.

A good example of the biographical approach is Richard Westfall's recent study of Isaac Newton. This large book draws on a vast literature and provides an excellent example of the *contextual* approach to the science of the past. Westfall does not make the old mistake of abstracting the physics from the context of theology, philosophy and alchemy which loomed large in Newton's mental world. A political dimension emerges not so much in Newton's own life as in the uses which are alleged to have been made by Church and State in eighteenth-century Britain of the Newtonian system.

But history of science must be more than the study of individuals. Historians of science have recently been increasingly concerned with institutions. From the seventeenth century onwards men organised themselves into societies, of which the most famous were the Royal Society of London (1660) and the Paris Academy of Sciences (1666). State patronage of science raises interesting questions and there is a striking contrast in the relation between science and government in Britain and France. Searching questions are being asked about the membership of scientific societies, whether on an amateur part-time basis, as in the British Association, or in a more élitist and professional way, as in the French Academy.

If ladies and gentlemen in nineteenth-century Britain turned to science for recreation, what did they expect to find? Was it a reassuring picture buttressing the existing social order and the established church? And what of the Mechanics Institutes? Here, as elsewhere, there are so many interesting questions to ask and only a handful of specialists engaged in finding answers. Unlike political history, history of science is a comparatively new field. It needs more people with some training in history and an interest in the history of ideas and the applications of science.

FURTHER READING

Barnes, B., *Scientific Knowledge and Sociological Theory* (London, 1974); *Interests and the Growth of Knowledge* (London, 1977); Barnes, B. and Shapin, S., *Natural Order: Historical Studies of Scientific Culture* (London and Beverly Hills, 1979); Bloor, D., *Knowledge and Social Imagery* (London, 1976); *Wittgenstein: A Social Theory of Knowledge* (London, 1983); Burtt, E. A., *The Metaphysical Foundations of Modern Political Science* (second edition, London, 1932); Collins, H. M., *Changing Order: Replication and Induction in Scientific Practice* (London, 1985); Cooter, R., *The Cultural Meaning of Popular Science: Phrenology and the Organization of Consent in Nineteenth-Century Britain* (Cambridge, 1984); Corsi, P. and Weindling, P. (eds), *Information Sources in the History of Science and Medicine* (London, 1983); Crosland, M. P., *Gay-Lussac, Scientist and Bourgeois* (Cambridge, 1978); Durbin, P. T. (ed.), *A Guide to the Culture of Science, Technology and Medicine* (New York, 1980); Fleck, L., *Genesis and Development of a Scientific Fact* (Basel, 1935, eds Trenn,

T. J. and Merton, R. K., Chicago, 1979); Grim, P. (ed.), *Philosophy of Science and the Occult* (Albany, 1982); Hahn, R., *The Anatomy of a Scientific Institution: The Paris Academy of Sciences, 1666–1803* (California, 1971); Hanen, M. P. *et al* (eds), *Science and Pseudo-Science and Society* (Waterloo, Ontario, 1980); Knight, D. M., *Sources for the History of Science* (London, 1975); Kuhn, T. S., *The Essential Tension: Selected Studies in Scientific Tradition and Change* (Chicago, 1977); Schaffer, S. and Shapin, S., *Leviathan and the Air-Pump: Hobbes, Boyle and the Experimental Life* (Princeton, 1985); Wallis, R. (ed.), *On the Margins of Science: the Social Construction of Rejected Knowledge* (Keele, 1979); Westfall, R. S., *Never at Rest: a Biography of Isaac Newton* (Cambridge, 1978); Whitehead, A. N., *Science and the Modern World* (1925, London, 1985); Young, R. M., *Darwin's Metaphor: Nature's Place in Victorian Culture* (Cambridge, 1984); *History of Science* (Journal, London, 1962–).

THE CONTRIBUTORS

Roger Cooter is Research Fellow at the Institute of Science and Technology, University of Manchester, and author of *The Cultural Meaning of Popular Science* (Cambridge, 1985).

Maurice Crosland is Professor of the History of Science at the University of Kent, Canterbury, and author of *Gay-Lussac, Scientist and Bourgeois* (Cambridge, 1978).

Roy Porter is Senior Lecturer in the History of Science at the Wellcome Institute for the History of Medicine and author of *English Society in the Eighteenth Century* (London, 1982).

Simon Schaffer is Lecturer in the History of Science at St John's, Cambridge, and author with Steven Shapin of *Leviathan and the Air-Pump: Hobbes, Boyle and the Experimental Life* (Princeton, 1985).

Steven Shapin is Lecturer in the Social History of Science at the Science Studies Unit, University of Edinburgh, and co-author of *Leviathan and the Air-Pump*.

Robert M. Young was Chief Consultant to 'Crucible: Science in Society' for Channel 4, and author of *Darwin's Metaphor: Nature's Place in Victorian Culture* (Cambridge, 1984).

7. WHAT IS
WOMEN'S HISTORY . . . ?

*Writing women back into the record? Rewriting the past?
Ghetto history? The study of the dynamics of power and
oppression? The discovery of heroines? Gender analysis?
What is women's history?*

Olwen Hufton

It is perhaps a salutary exercise in the midst of writing a book whose
scope is as breathtakingly wide as *Women in European Society 1500–
1800* to define what one is about. For me, a history of women implies
a triple commitment. The first and most obvious is to discern
women's past rôle and situation – in this instance to locate them in
the social, economic, religious, political and psychological *monde
immobile* of traditional society. The second is to give the history of
the period a 'gender dimension': less grandly, to suggest relevant
areas or issues in the period under review where the attitudes or
position of women, differentiated perhaps by class or national
group, influenced the course of events, and hence to make clear that
to write history without reference to gender is to distort the vision.
Thirdly, women did not live in society in isolation. Indeed, much of
the evidence about them in the period which my book covers, given
differential literacy rates, was compiled or invented by men and
rests on male assumptions. In examining some of these, we are
looking not merely at how men conceived 'the sex' but also
themselves. At this point, the history of women becomes the history
of mentalities.

When Peter Laslett reviewed Scott and Tilly, *Women, Work and
Family* (R. W. Holt, 1978), he pointed out, very pertinently, that
there was no simple, single record of a past woman to represent all
women; that experience varied according to class, area and time.
That said, heaped upon Western European woman in this period
was a common, weighty, ideological heritage to which Judaic
philosophy (Eve as evil, woman as the greater sinner, unclean
during the menstrual phase, unworthy of full participation in
religious life), Christian doctrine, Greek science and philosophy,
Roman law and the traditions of violent agrarian societies where
physical strength was at a premium, had each made a contribution.

The result was a gloomy view of woman as a defective being, the 'botched male' of the Greek tradition whose main characteristics were her irrationality (the Greek for uterus and hysteria being virtually the same), lust (before the second half of the eighteenth century it was held that woman's physical composition made her more demanding of sex than men), obsession with luxurious apparel and her own fair form and garrulity. Such were her most conspicuous attributes. Such a person's only hope was firm governance by husband or father. How was such a view modified or redressed? Was it by the Reformation, the Enlightenment which threw out notions of a God-ordained society, by literary traditions acknowledging a *femme forte*, by increasing female literacy which allowed some women to seize the pen in their own defence, by a growing consciousness amongst eighteenth-century male novelists that increasingly they were dependent on a female audience, or by theological revisionism in recognising the growing feminisation of religion? Where and for what reasons did the voice of ripost become more than a whimper? How much of this legacy was left and where by 1800? How did women live with this burden upon them?

The gap between theory and practice can be great. Ideas need to be tested against the practicalities of existence (modified by area and class) for women in traditional societies. Demography and family history have both been growth areas in recent years. The first has provided an excellent *factual* framework: how many married, at what age, to whom, for how long and with what issue? The second has endowed us with a confused and inadequate set of hypotheses about the qualitative aspects of marriage and parenthood, creating a 'black-legend' of women in traditional societies as affectionless, zombie-like child-beaters. The historian of women needs to use the demographic data and explain the implications for women of a situation in which the numbers who married and the age at which they did so depended upon economic performance so that in hard times the numbers of spinsters and widows rose. From the material of family history she needs to ask how much of the legend is grounded in fantasy? How many mythological images of women in the past are the creation of the historians?

The importance of economic factors in marriage is rightly universally stressed; and of enormous relevance to the history of women is an appreciation of their role in the European economy. Agrarian societies can rarely absorb all their woman-power in work on the land. In traditional societies, as commercial wealth expanded, a great reservoir of young women was taken into domestic service. Others turned to industrial employment. For every man involved in the production of any textile there were ten times as many women. The industrial performance of traditional society – at its most sophisticated level, a world of beautiful textiles, lace, silks, embroideries, ribbons – rested on an ill-paid female workforce. Ill-paid because the wages women could command were based on the assumption that a male figure paid for the roof above their heads and that their only concern was with subsistence. Precluded from craft apprenticeships by guilds and restrictive practices, women pushed their way into sections of the garment trades (as seamstresses and milliners) too exposed to the vagaries of fashion for male tastes. When times were hard and the numbers of single women rose, the archives of poverty expose the spinster, the widow and dependent brood as the pauper figures of the past. A history of poverty is invariably largely a history of women.

Recognition must also be made of a spinster predicament in higher social echelons where families lacked the means to provide all their daughters with dowries and the women, as intelligent as their brothers, faced the limited outlets of governess, companion, nurse or turned to literary endeavour which rarely made them self-supporting. Hence, from the seventeenth century onwards, in Britain and the Netherlands at least, we can locate an articulate, discontented sector. In Catholic societies, the charitable and teaching orders may have served to absorb some of these women and hence discontent was more muted. It is, however, significant that teaching, nursing, tending the old, prison care and running orphanages were women's work whether or not a conventual framework existed.

The social life of European women in the past pivoted on the market, the washplace, the well and the church. In much of Europe no women other than prostitutes enjoyed a tavern-based social life and even in parts of Britain and Flanders only working-class women could afford to be seen there. The woman of any social standing who was not a part of court society had little life outside the home except that offered by the church. Small wonder that in religious movements across the continent we find the keen involvement of women. In Protestant sects some demanded 'a voice equal to that of men' – they sought religious parity long before political parity. They were Quakers and Methodists, indeed the composition of the crowd surrounding Wesley was as heavily female as that surrounding Christ on the cross. The cult of the Rosary appealed particularly to women because it belonged in the home and the workplace. We find them in Catholic Europe hostile to any change which disrupted the religious outlet. When the French Revolution demolished the church, women reconstructed it. They became the focus of protest. Their rôle in the market made them the essential part of consumer protest movements. Indeed as long as protest focused on prices rather than wages, the role of women was primordial.

Even by the end of the period notions of sharing political power amongst anything other than a narrow male élite were limited and essays in male democracy during the Revolution proved abortive. We have to find women in politics as lineage pawns, their marriages part of treaty arrangements, as part of the web of political intrigue found in absolutist courts, as mistresses of kings and politicians and as hostesses of élites.

Historians of women in industrial society have posited, as the product of industrial capitalism, a downgrading process. At some time, it is argued, women worked harmoniously in the home by their husbands' sides: the lady of the manor brewed, baked and taught her servants to read and was not yet a social parasite. So far I have found no lasting *bon vieux temps*. I see women perpetually in the meanest jobs and dependent upon upturns in the economy to permit them even a limited *entrée* into more skilled work: at the next downturn they return to whence they had begun. If change permitted the lady of the manor to read and criticise she was as well employed as in the bakery. I discern, over time, limited revisionism in how women were talked about and even treated in law. When I see seventeenth- and eighteenth-century women demanding religious or economic equality, I find myself resentful of a definition of first-wave feminism which locates struggle in the late nineteenth century. I find that more than anything else I am writing about a survival process which in the main weighed more heavily on women than men. If I can generate some appreciation of that struggle, of such rewards as were to be had, and of what women cared about in times past, I shall, in my own esteem at least, have written women's history.

Natalie Zemon Davis

Women's history, to begin with means including women in the historical record. If one is looking at the history of agriculture, one sorts out women's work from men's when these are different, and talks of women's training, tools, tasks and customs. If one is writing about a political movement, one asks whether it has women among its supporters and organisers, 'women's issues' among its concerns, and women among the writers and readers of its pamphlets. In this most elementary sense, women's history is a very old genre. Women worthies have been memorialised even before Christine de Pisan wrote her *City of Ladies*; queens, abbesses and female saints and literary figures have had their biographers; histories of prostitution, midwifery, witchcraft and salons were all written in the nineteenth century. What is significant about the contemporary inquiry is the extension of the question 'and what about the women?' to all areas of historical research – even to those where at first glance it may seem hard to find evidence. Archives and libraries are searched and old texts reread for new meanings, and the result can be a stunning book like Olwen Hufton's *The Poor of Eighteenth-Century France*, where women's economy of makeshifts and impro-visation casts light on the situation and mentality of the lower orders. Similarly, the search for women has been one of the impulses behind historical engagement with other current topics: the family and childrearing, domestic life and space, sexuality, authorship, and symbolic representations.

At its most substantial women's history shows what *difference* it makes to historical interpretation when the category of the sexes is included. Or we might also say when the analysis of 'gender' is included, expanding that word beyond grammar to a social and cultural meaning. The history of socialism looks different when Barbara Taylor tells us in *Eve and the New Jerusalem* of the significance of the Utopian experiments for women. The issues in the French Revolution are clarified when the varieties of women's positions are examined separately from the men's; when the threatening feminist republicanism of a few women's clubs is contrasted with the patriarchical republicanism of the Jacobins; when one reflects on why critics, including women, denounced the Old Regime as 'effeminate' and called for 'manly virtue' from *le beau sexe*.

As these examples suggest, women's history must always be comparative, women's experience compared to men's, women's experience in one class compared to that of another, women's experience compared across boundaries of religion and country. Even when the subject matter concentrates on women, as in *The Land before Her*, Annette Kolodny's fine study of texts by American frontierswomen, the comparative perspective is drawn upon, 'the romance of the wilderness cultivator' comprehensible only as it competes with 'the heroic mythology of the wilderness hunter', fantasy comprehensible only as it is contrasted with experience. In the course of such comparative consideration over the past twenty years, women's history has fallen into the same two modes as all other kinds of historical writing: the mode that looks for universals in female experience (woman is to man as nature is to culture, as domestic is to public; women as always resisters or as always victims) and the mode that looks for varieties in female experience. Though both elements are always present in historical inquiry – the past would be opaque if we could not at least recognise what a woman was in another time and place and would be boring if it were always the same thing over and over again – my own preference is for variety. The evidence suggests what a range there has been in sexual systems, in sexual economies and sexual symbols, in certain periods the lines between the sexes drawn quite sharply and in others quite fluid, with associated consequences for the division of labour and the distribution of power.

What is happening to 'women's history', of course, is that it is being extended to men. Sexual identity is an historical construction for both sexes, and it is surely formed differently when a society allows citizens to be simultaneously lovers of boys, husbands and fathers from when a society offers free men only the choice between being celibate priests and married warriors. If W. L. Wiley's *Gentleman of Renaissance France* were written today, it would focus not only on what it was to be gentle rather than common or vulgar, but on what it was to be manly – in regard to women, to other men and to the self. Women's history is a way to renew the history of both sexes, to give us a new understanding of the possibilities of the past.

Sally Humphreys

There are three possible ways of defining women's history, which in the early stages of the use of the term tended to overlap, but which now need separating: history by women, history about women, history written from a feminist point of view. In its early stages 'women's history', like 'women's studies', was closely linked to the consciousness – raising polemics of the women's movement. But there are now signs of increasing awareness that history written exclusively about, by and for women can never achieve more than ghetto significance. As Elizabeth Fox-Genovese put it in a recent article, we have to think about 'Placing Women's History in History' (*New Left Review*, 133, 1982). Women's history, like other forms of 'history from below' such as 'People's history', faces the challenge of showing that it can transform and enrich the mainstream historical tradition which it accuses of bias, rather than merely filling in some interstitial gaps in the picture.

To do this, in my opinion, women's history has to define its subject-matter as the history of conceptions of gender (i.e. of 'men' and 'women' as social, not natural beings) and of the social relationships and experiences to which gender ideologies are tied, rather than as the history of 'women' in isolation. Conceptions of feminine 'nature' are bound up with conceptions of masculine 'nature', two sides of the same coin. And the advantages do not all work one way. In my view, our current conceptions of gender and division of labour exclude men just as much as women from worthwhile areas of experience and forms of self-expression.

I would therefore like to see 'women's history' take a less esoteric and polemical tone, and widen its area of investigation. Not because I see academic history as an objective, theoretical activity which has to be kept pure from the distortions inherent in political practice, but because much of the polemical writing associated with the women's movement seems to me muddle-headed and unlikely to produce helpful results. There is a conflict of aims between those who want to establish equality for women in the public sphere by arguing that women are quite capable of conforming to current standards of male behaviour, and those who want to transform the public sphere by imposing on it the values currently associated with women. Only a radical reconsideration of the way we divide life between nature and culture, masculine and feminine qualities and activities, public and private life, work and not-work, will clarify this situation.

But what can historical research contribute? First of all, a critique of currently received ideas about what is 'natural' in gender and the division of labour between the sexes, which can often show that what now seems natural is a recent historical development. A history of psychoanalytic practice and theory and of the conditions which produced it is one of the urgent tasks here. Secondly, an analysis of changes in gender relations which shows how they relate to other social factors, and especially to class relations. While it is surely true that women, and men, have common interests as a sex which cut across class barriers, it is also true that changes in gender relations have often had very different effects in different classes. There has been much interesting research recently on the way in which women's involvement in voluntary philanthropic work in the nineteenth century, while reinforcing the trend towards confining women to domestic concerns, nevertheless allowed middle-class women a limited access to the public sphere, while simultaneously subordinating working-class women to increased control and interference from outside. Middle-class and working-class conceptions of masculinity bear a strong imprint of class differentiation as well as gender differentiation; and recent studies of teenage sub-cultures have shown that they are determined both by gender and by social class.

Even an historian of ancient Greece can contribute to the debate. Our conceptions of the division between public and private spheres and its relation to gender owe much to classical Athens and the influence of Greek models on western conceptions of public life and democratic politics in the eighteenth and nineteenth centuries. In a recent collection of essays (*The Family, Women and Death: comparative studies*) I have tried to explore the historical conditions which made the separation of public and private spheres possible in classical Athens and the implicit criticism which the ideological subordination of the private sphere provoked from poets, from philosophers and from ordinary Athenians, whose tombstones show them preferring to be remembered in their private roles, in a timeless representation of family intimacy. We have no statement by an Athenian woman of her reaction to these changes, but Sophocles' *Antigone* provides a truly classic portrayal of the contradictions of a culture which expects men to think only of public affairs and women to confine themselves to domestic life.

Angela V. John

Imagine opening any reputable book on social history and finding an index entry entitled 'Men'. Such a category, quite likely to be synonymous with the book's subject-matter, would seem superfluous and absurd. Yet it still appears 'promising' if one of those books contains a number of index references to 'Women'.

For some historians this indicates that a discrepancy exists between the experiences of people in the past and the partial representation of some of them in the present and so illustrates a need for women's history. This, it is argued, should be more than simply the history of women since an awareness of injustices in both present and past invests it with a particular empathy and potency, alerting us to the dangers of automatically assuming that the interests and priorities in women's lives are the same as or less valid than those of men.

The British coalmining industry of the nineteenth and early twentieth century demonstrates the challenge and problems of women's history. With few exceptions it has been portrayed as a study of minerals and machinery by men, about men and for men. Whether from the perspectives of social, labour or business historians, leaders and institutions have been revered. The focus has been on the place of production, the face. Surface workers, employed in less dramatic and dangerous conditions, have therefore received little attention despite representing a fifth of the total workforce at its height. They were men relegated by age, accident or disease, or lads acquiring experience before working underground. They were women with no prospects and little status. Though sorting coal at picking belts demanded dexterity and skill (and was not exclusively 'women's work'), their employment was viewed as an end in itself, unskilled and worth half a man's wage. It filled a gap between school and marriage though many remained single and dependent on pit work. Others returned later as wives or widows of miners disabled or killed. Whereas for men, mining spelt masculinity and strength, for women it denoted the antithesis of the qualities most respected in the female sex. Victorian pit lasses were denounced as unsexed, immoral Amazons. Their day's turn was followed not by a night in the pub or institute (a jealously guarded male preserve) but by a second shift of housework. Families were large and wives' and daughters' work was needed, especially since dirt came home before the advent of pithead baths.

Women's mining history has its own time-table and chronology. For example the development of the Welsh steam-coal trade (1870s), with its opportunities for male miners, meant no corresponding bonanza for women workers. Wartime, however, doubled the numbers of British pit women though their subsequent displacement and eventual unchallenged disappearance from mining adds another dimension to their chronology, so separate from the men's.

Women miners have occasionally entered the historical consciousness. Schoolchildren still learn about the horrors facing Victorian women and children underground, a social evil. Yet women had been miners for centuries, conditions were less primitive than previously and numbers declining by 1842. Moreover many women worked illegally (and with greater vulnerability) for years after the 1842 law cleared the Victorian guilt conscience. In contrast, the successful struggle of surface women to retain their right to work in the 1880s (and again in 1911) has not been analysed as a *cause célèbre*. This story was not documented until the 1970s, another time of concern with women's legal rights. The lack of previous historical attention (though in 1928 the feminist Ray Strachey had briefly noted the Victorian campaign) is all the more remarkable since the pit lasses had become a test case for the right of working women to resist protective legislation and involved prominent Victorian suffragists, trade unionists, employers, politicians and philanthropists. They bequeathed a rich and varied store of primary evidence.

In redirecting attention to such neglected concerns, women's history requires sensitivity to contextualisation, resisting an exaggeration of female influence and the substitution of alternative heroines. It should question both the workings of patriarchy and the pervasiveness of class. Pit lasses were neither magically modernising themselves nor were they passive victims. Though active in their cause, ultimately their case was channelled via those possessing the power and status to influence society.

To appreciate the lives of mining women we also need to push beyond rediscovering the public protests. Yet voices become less distinct as we unravel the intricacies of daily life, especially since they lack their own memoirs and receive at best only fleeting testimonies in miners' autobiographies (though oral history can remedy this for some). We require a finely tuned ear to listen to their voices, paying attention to language, to what is derisively dismissed as 'women's gossip', locating networks and forms of protest, identifying both the constraints and the strengths of women's lives. By straining to hear the meanings behind the silences as well as the shouts we can perhaps get a little closer to appreciating the present and the differing priorities of the past for women and for men, thus moving beyond a concentration on women's history alone. Questioning values and assumptions and concerned with sexual difference, feminist historians have also identified a need for examination of the meanings of masculinity so that gender can be conceptualised more rigorously.

A book index can move beyond entries for one or indeed both sexes to recognise, as well as concepts such as class, the centrality of gender to historical understanding, thereby challenging the boundaries of historical theory and practice.

Linda Gordon

Women's history is by definition critical history. That is widely understood, but some commentators misunderstand or, perhaps defensively, trivialise the content of its critique. The earliest works of this wave of women's history protested against exclusions from the historical record. These exclusions created deformations and falsehoods, not mere omissions. (Consider the phrase 'universal suffrage,' consistently applied to manhood suffrage or the judgement that certain societies were 'democratic' when half their populations had neither legal rights nor representation.) Women's historians quickly moved beyond correcting a 'bias' to arguing with the very definition of history, asking for new definitions of power and influence to include those who less often held political office, wrote books, memos or treaties. Women's history is not 'remedial' in the sense that it can be dispensed with as soon as we can retrain historians to a fair-minded inclusion of both sexes (although even that minimal goal, despite great progress towards it, remains distant). Women's history questions what has been labelled important, not only by historians, but also by citizens. Women's historians protest the domination of history-making as well as history-writing by men. So long as there remains sexual inequality, women's history exists in relation to an active or dormant women's rights struggle, even when that relation is critical or defensive.

One must not distinguish women's history thereby from other more traditional histories, however. Interpretations of the past, however well crafted and critically appraised by the individual historian, always serve some present interests. The leaving out of women, the leaving out of the kinds of activities that women do, the lower status of 'social history' than diplomatic history – these are ideological artefacts.

Women's history is being defined in practice, which is perhaps what makes the field today so productive. Probably the largest single reason for its vitality is that its rationale challenges it to explore institutions, social formations and source materials not previously included in the scope of history. Many 'women's historians' work on topics that include but are not limited to women, conceptualising major historical processes differently because women are now a part of them, historicising activities not previously seen as historical because they were assumed to be 'natural.' I am studying the history of family violence – child abuse, wife-beating, sexual assault – as an example of the problem of social control. In discussing transformations in gender and family relations in a nineteenth-century town, Mary Ryan reveals new aspects of the formation of the 'middle class'. Judith Walkowitz has unravelled the fabric of conflicts over the British Contagious Diseases Acts to examine the separate threads of sexual and class, religious, reform and political dynamics of late nineteenth-century England. Architect-historian Dolores Hayden recovered a lost history of plans for community living motivated by women's imagination and resistance to the conditions of individualised housework.

The new women's history has changed extraordinarily quickly. We are each others' sharpest critics, in part because of the velocity with which a women's social movement has spread and challenged old verities, in part because the work is new, and rapidly developing standards, methods, and a body of classics. Recent work soon becomes outdated, by new findings as well as more sophisticated methodological and theoretical standards. Professionalisation (especially advanced in the United States) has costs – it is harder for amateurs to dare to enter the field, and easier for technically proficient but trivial work to win recognition. But there are also strengths to this escalation of standards. There is a demand, evident among college students and political activists, that historical work avoid reductionism and simplistic, monocausal explanations, and grapple with many categories of analysis simultaneously – gender, sex, sexual preference, class, race, profession, nationality, religion. The documentation and denunciation of women's suppression, a task that appeared sufficient fifteen years ago, seems now virtually pointless to many historians and readers unless it is integrated with discussions of the resistance, compromises, and ambiguities with which women actually negotiated relations between the sexes.

Above all much of the new women's history contains challenges to determinism. In my own work on birth control and family violence, in Judith Leavitt's work on the history of childbirth, in Alice Kessler-Harris' work on women's wage-earning, in Nancy Cott's and Carroll Smith-Rosenberg's work on women's networks, women's historians like many labour historians are showing that even conditions of domination are the outcomes of conflict, not unilaterally imposed oppressions.

Perhaps the most common misconception about women's history is that it is new. In fact there was a burst of historical scholarship about women in the early twentieth century when a first generation of educated women sought to correct an historical record that had left them out. Americans such as Edith Abbott, Helen Sumner, Rolla Tryon, the English Alice Clark, Wanda Neff and Ivy Pinchbeck produced sophisticated analyses of the impact of industrialisation on women, for example, which have not been superseded. Yet in my professional training in history, I never heard any of these names. The fortunes of these historians and their work followed those of the women's rights movement as a whole: the weakening of that movement in the period 1920–60 allowed for the virtual suppression of their work. Women historians of my generation taught ourselves women's history, searching through libraries, finding these splendid books on the shelves of old university libraries, literally untouched for decades. The process left many of us with a wariness towards the possiblity of such suppression, and a determination to prevent its recurrence.

FURTHER READING

Boswell, J., *Christianity, Social Tolerance and Homosexuality: Gay People in Western Europe from the Beginning of Christianity to the Fourteenth Century* (Chicago, 1980); Bray, A., *Homosexuality in Renaissance England* (London, 1982); Bynum, C., *Holy Feast and Holy Fast: The Religious Significance of Food to Medieval Women* (Berkley and Los Angeles, 1987); Carroll, B. A. (ed.), *Liberating Women's History* (Illinois, 1976); Davis, N. Z., *Society and Culture in Early Modern France* (Stanford, 1975); Donzelot, J., *The Policing of Families* (London, 1980); Fox-Genovese, E., 'Placing Women's History in History' in *New Left Review*, 133 (1982); Hanawalt, B. (ed.), *Women and Work in Preindustrial Europe* (Bloomington, Indiana, 1985); Hall, S. and Jefferson, T. (eds), *Resistance through Rituals* (London, 1976); Howell, M., *Women, Production and Patriarchy in late Medieval Cities* (Chicago, 1986); Hufton, O., *The Poor of Eighteenth-Century France,*

1750–1789 (Oxford, 1974); Humphreys, S. (ed.), *The Family, Women and Death* (London, 1983); John, A. V., *By the Sweat of Their Brow: Women Workers at Victorian Coalmines* (London, 1984); Klapisch-Zuber, C., *Women, Family and Ritual in Renaissance Italy*, trans. Cochrane, L. (Chicago, 1985); Labalme, P. A. (ed.), *Beyond Their Sex: Learned Women of the European Past* (New York, 1980); Larner, C., *Enemies of God: The Witch-hunt in Scotland* (London, 1981); MacFarlane, A., *The Family Life of Ralph Josselin: A Seventeenth-Century Clergyman. An Essay in Historical Anthropology* (Cambridge, 1970); Maclean, I., *The Renaissance Notion of Women: A Study in the Fortunes of Scholasticism and Medical Science in European Intellectual Life* (Cambridge, 1980); Otis, L., *Prostitution in Medieval Society. The History of an Urban Institution in Languedoc* (Chicago, 1985); Pizan, C de., *The Book of the City of Ladies* (Harmondsworth edition 1985); Poster, M., *A Critical Theory of the Family* (London, 1977); Scott, J., 'Women in History' in *Past and Present*, 101 (1983); Slater, M., *Family Life in the Seventeenth-Century. The Verneys of Claydon House* (London, 1984); Stone, L., *The Family, Sex and Marriage in Renaissance England 1500–1800* (London, 1977); Summers, A., 'A Home from Home. Women's Philanthropic Work in the Nineteenth Century' in Burman, S. (ed.), *Fit Work for Women* (Beckenham, 1979); Thomas, K., 'Women in Civil War Sects' in *Past and Present*, 13, (1985); Tilly, L. and Scott, J. W., *Women, Work and Family* (New York, 1978); Tolson, A., *The Limits of Masculinity* (London, 1977); Verdier, Y., *Façons de Dire, Façons de Faire. La Laveuse, la Courtière, la Cuisinière* (Paris, 1979); *The Memoirs of Glückel of Hameln*, trans. Marvin Lowenthal (New York, 1977); *Llafur*: The Journal of the Society for the Study of Welsh Labour History, Vol. 4, No. 1 (issue on Women's History).

THE CONTRIBUTORS

Natalie Zemon Davis is Professor of History at Princeton University and author of *The Return of Martin Guerre* (Harvard, 1983, Harmondsworth, 1985).

Linda Gordon is Professor of History at the Univesity of Wisconsin and author of *Cruelty, Love and Dependence: Family Violence and Social Control, Boston 1880–1960* (New York, 1985).

Olwen Hufton is Professor of Modern History at the University of Reading and author of *Europe: Privilege and Protest, 1730–89* (London, 1985).

Sally Humphreys is Professor of History at the University of Michigan and author of *The Family, Women and Death* (London, 1983).

Angela V. John is Senior Lecturer in History at Thames Polytechnic and editor of *Unequal Opportunities. Women's Employment in England 1800–1918* (Oxford, 1985).

8. WHAT IS
THE HISTORY OF ART . . . ?

*The authentication and dating of brushstrokes? An analysis
of the development of style? A chronicle of patronage and
taste? A focus of debate about definitions of culture? A gloss
on connoisseurship? A reflection of the realities of society?
What is the history of art?*

Alex Potts

A history of the visual arts, defined simply as a chronological
description of the various objects we now classify as art, would be a
pretty marginal affair, probably of less general interest than a
history of machinery, or a history of clothing. It would certainly be a
history that remained on the fringes of what most people recognise
as the central concerns of life. A history of art begins to look a little
more interesting where it claims that art has a symbolic value, and
that visual artefacts reflect important attitudes and 'realities' of the
society in which they were produced.

Such claims were first advanced explicitly during the Enlightenment, most notably in Winckelmann's famous *History of the Art of
Antiquity*, published in 1764. With Winckelmann, art was conceived, not just as a category of visual representations that provoked
pleasurable responses, but as a medium for defining ourselves and
our engagement with the material world – in Hegel's words,
Winckelmann, in characterising art in the way he did, invented a
'new organ of the human spirit'. At the same time, artefacts of the
past were interpreted as eloquent signs of the general character of
the society that had produced them. In the words of another
contemporary, the Comte de Caylus, a collection of antiquities,
classified according to place and date of origin, would provide a
'picture of all the centuries'. Similar preoccupations are still active in
the study of the history of art, but cast in a much more negative
mould.

Ideas of art and the aesthetic have at no time attracted such
intense scholarly scrutiny as now; yet arguments for their actual
significance rarely ring true. The more convincing studies are
concerned with the ideological interests which lie behind traditional
mythologies of art, or with questions about why art might have
mattered in the past. Similarly, the idea that the meanings of art are

anchored in social and political life, that art history should be conceived as an integral part of general history, has rarely been so widely accepted; yet attempts to ascribe definite social and political meanings to visual images usually meet with scepticism. The fruitful art historical analyses, rather than explaining the exact meaning of an image, demonstrate how futile it is to try and fix the varied and often ill-defined meanings it could have for different audiences in different contexts. Interpreted as bits of historical evidence illustrating what a past society was like, visual artefacts tend to function as intriguing images onto which we are all free to project whatever historical fantasies we wish. The central concerns of art historical study have not always been so intensely problematic. But the paradoxes involved can be traced back to the formation of a modern conception of the history of art in the eighteenth and nineteenth centuries.

Jacob Burckhardt's definition of the Renaissance as a distinct phase in the history of Western European culture obviously owes a lot to his study of Italian Renaissance art. Yet when he came to write his *Civilization of the Renaissance in Italy*, published in 1860, he did not discuss the visual arts, and defined his conception of Italian Renaissance culture entirely from written sources. The Renaissance is still represented most vividly for many people by Italian Renaissance art, just as Modernism seems most clearly exemplified in modern art. But it is only at a highly symbolic level that an abstract painting, say, can be interpreted as symptomatic of tendencies within modern culture as a whole. If the history of art has encouraged a division of general history into phases or periods, specialised studies of art seem to offer few concrete insights into the larger social and political factors, or the prevailing day-to-day attitudes and ways of life, that might characterise such periods.

Yet interest in the past is to a considerable extent formed by responses to visual artefacts, and the study of the visual arts is not as marginal as its ostensible function serving the art market and tourist industry would seem to imply. Art continues to be a focus of debate about definitions of culture – though what matters much more in practical terms is the use of visual imagery in the media and film, even for the minority of the rich and powerful who make the art scene their hobby.

Winckelmann's history of Greek and Roman art, the publication that effectively put the modern study of the history of art on the map, was based on artefacts that featured in the day-to-day life of only a tiny circle of antiquarians and collectors of antique sculpture in eighteenth-century Rome. Yet the book seemed to break the bounds of the interests of this exclusive and peripheral social group, largely by virtue of claims about the value of art and its history that seem highly suspect, yet gripping, today.

John House

The history of art is facing a particular problem at the moment: we need to find ways of relating the detailed discussion of works of art to a wide-ranging historical analysis of the conditions, and preconditions, of their making. I am one of many who are dissatisfied with the most traditional forms of object-based art history, which seek as their prime goal to identify the works of a particular hand or to analyse the development of 'styles' as self-contained, isolated phenomena. In stark reaction against this is an historical analysis which focuses on the institutional frameworks within which works of art have been made and on the presuppositions (the unspoken assumptions as well as the declared systems of belief) which underpin their making. These issues are crucial; but I am worried by the way in which some such discussions find no place for the analysis of the particular characteristics of individual works of art.

I do not want to treat works of art as hallowed objects of reverence, but rather as artefacts which have a specific history, in their making, and in their reception and use from then until now. I am interested in gaining a more wide-ranging view of the art of a place and period by juxtaposing and comparing the diverse works of art from that context, and by relating the appearance of these works and their trajectory through space and time to the circumstances and preconditions of their making and consumption. Necessarily, too, we must acknowledge that the historian's access to the past is indirect, since it is filtered through subsequent events, and that it is partial in both senses of the word: fragmentary, and inseparable from the historian's own values and beliefs.

I am currently beginning a study of realism in nineteenth-century painting. This has been triggered by a frustration with accounts of realism in painting which appeal to 'reality' and 'objectivity' as their base. Realist enterprises took so many forms in the nineteenth century that no unitary base can make sense of them all; but, more significantly, the appeal to 'objectivity' short-circuits the ways in which ideas about the 'real' are encoded in a work of art, and the purposes and interests these serve. In the long term my research will seek to dovetail verbal with visual evidence: it will examine on the one hand the critical debates around the idea of realism and around the very varied types of painting which were taken in under the realist umbrella in the nineteenth century; and on the other hand it will analyse the pictorial devices and techniques by which paintings sought to encode ideas of the real and actual, treating pictorial composition and technique alike as types of rhetoric which were deployed in particular contexts and to particular ends.

Essential to this analysis is a study of art institutions, especially contexts of exhibition and sale; in big public exhibitions like the Paris Salon, particular sets of expectations and frameworks of classification evolved, which conditioned the artists' strategies. The 'realism' of Courbet's and Manet's big exhibition paintings, for instance, can only be understood by examining the contexts in which the paintings were shown – both visual (the other paintings in the Salons of the period) and verbal (the categories and criteria by which they were classified and judged); their most controversial paintings were conceived as deliberate interventions into specific pictorial and critical contexts.

Contemporary art criticism is of central importance to the study of nineteenth-century painting, since it played a fundamental role in mediating between works of art and their public; it is in the dialogue between artists and critic, between presentation and reception, that one must seek evidence for the meanings which a work of art conveyed, or sought to convey, to its first viewers. But criticism cannot give us direct access to the paintings, for it has its own history and rhetoric: it is detailed comparative analysis of the paintings themselves which will allow us to focus most closely on the distinctive characteristics they presented in their original contexts.

The methodological underpinning for this work largely comes from outside art history: from literary theory and from social and intellectual history; it is in these fields that the questions with which I am concerned have been more searchingly asked. The history of art must use the lessons drawn from these other subjects in order to develop its identity as a discipline – I am convinced it *is* a discipline! The subject needs a theoretical base, but this must be harnessed to the detailed specific applications which will enrich our understanding of the functions that art has served in history. Finally, we must never lose sight of the relevance of our analyses of the past to a critical understanding of the uses to which culture is put in our society today.

Charles Hope

In the early years of this century most art historians were principally interested in two types of problem. The first was to establish the authorship and date of works of art, the second to analyse changes of style both in the careers of individual artists and as a more general process. In other words, the focus was very largely on art as an autonomous phenomenon, rather than on the social circumstances surrounding its production; and the skills required were principally those of the connoisseur and the critic. Recently, the emphasis has shifted. The analysis of style still figures very largely in the teaching of art history, but much more attention is now paid to the study of patronage, taste and iconography. This has led to changes in method, especially to a greater interest in archival research and in the use of literary texts. In terms of the methods employed and the questions that are asked, art history now seems much more like other types of history.

In one major respect, however, it is bound to remain distinctive, since any historical study involving works of art necessarily involves aesthetic judgements. This applies most obviously in questions of attribution and dating, which are fundamental to almost any type of further enquiry in the history of art. Except for some of the art of this century, the documentary evidence about such issues is usually incomplete, and has to be supplemented by old-fashioned connoisseurship. To many people this seems something rather mysterious. In fact, the term covers two quite separate processes. One is to identify, at least approximately, the authors of a very large range of works of art. The other is to make much more subtle differentiations of quality, to decide, for example, between an autograph painting and a product by an assistant or imitator, or to locate a specific work precisely within the context of a particular artist's output as a means of dating it.

These two types of activity require different skills. The first calls above all for an exceptional visual memory, the second for a special sensitivity to an individual artist's style. And anyone who is familiar with, for example, the scholarly literature on Renaissance art will very soon realise that many specialists in the field do not necessarily possess either of these skills to any great degree, and least of all the second. Thus until recently it was believed by several of the foremost authorities on Raphael that a large ceiling fresco by him was actually the work of a painter of very different character, Baldassare Peruzzi, while an altarpiece in the museum at Lille, which was widely assigned to Titian, supposedly working in his latest and most personal style, subsequently turned out to be by an obscure seventeenth-century Spanish artist named Diego Polo. This does not of course mean that connoisseurship is necessarily unreliable, but that anyone who studies the history of art needs to know their own limitations, as well as those of other scholars in the field.

It is quite often supposed, especially by those who specialise in connoisseurship, that other aspects of the subject do not call for the same degree of visual sensitivity. This is extremely questionable. For example, anyone who studies patterns of patronage and taste can hadly avoid considering the quality of works of art which particular patrons might have acquired, or trying to reconstruct that patron's response to such works. In the same way, any investigation of the subject-matter of a work of art, its iconography, is liable to go astray unless it takes account of the fact that artists were seldom required simply to illustrate stories or to represent visual symbols, but were also expected to produce something beautiful.

This is not to say that contracts, letters and contemporary texts, as well as scientific studies of technique and computerised databases, will not provide a vast amount of indispensable information to the art historian. But they will not provide all the answers to the questions that he is likely to ask, whether he studies art for its own sake or as part of a wider historical enquiry. It is because works of art are different from other artefacts of the past, because they demand an aesthetic response before they can be understood, that art history remains a distinctive discipline, which makes special demands not only on those who practise it, but also on anyone who wants to use its conclusions for other purposes. To a certain extent it is bound to be subjective in its methods and unrigorous in its conclusions, but this does not mean that those conclusions are necessarily unreliable.

Tom Gretton

What is art history? What is Art? In the late twentieth-century developed world enormous but ill-defined value is placed on 'art'. We use the word in many senses to many ends. The way in which we respond to what we call works of art is an important way of proclaiming our social status. The distinction we make between works of art and other man-made objects is an important way in which we come to accept the alienation implicit in the division of labour. We use 'art' to designate imprecise or traditional skills or bodies of knowledge. Even in History of Art the word embraces a subject matter wider than one might expect. The great paintings of old and new masters and mistresses are there, but so are LP album covers, printed biscuit tins, and other cultural forms not yet enshrined in National Galleries or the vaults of Pension Funds.

The questions which art historians are trained to raise may not be the most fruitful ones to ask of many sorts of pictures, and we may not want to assimilate objects such as Trade Union banners to a discipline which tends to explain the importance of images in terms of their transcendental, rather than their historical, value. For better or worse, however, research into the different sorts of jobs which different sorts of images did in the past tends to be done under the aegis of History of Art.

Images in the past, like images in the present, do a variety of different jobs, depending on their forms and their audience. They are part of the history of culture in the broad sense, of the whole range of artefacts, partly moral, partly institutional, and partly material, through which groups of humans deal with their environment. Culture in this wide sense does its work through the combination of all cultural forms, not through any one of them in isolation. Nonetheless, we can ask pertinent questions about the role of individual forms.

I am particularly interested in the popular imagery of England and France during the last century-and-a-half of the form's independent existence. Popular imagery was produced in western Europe from the early seventeenth century until the impact of new technologies and of new forms of social and economic organisation superseded it during the second half of the nineteenth century. Between about 1820 and 1860, there flourished, particularly in London and Paris, a trade in cheap single sheets, printed on one side of the paper only, usually at least as large as an open copy of the average size magazine today, often twice as large, on which texts and images were printed together. The subject-matter of these cheap prints varied, but concentrated on crime and punishment on the one hand, and on cautionary tales and religious subjects on the other. There were important differences between the prints produced in the two countries. These can help us to understand various aspects of the cultures of England and France, for example the different roles played by written and by figurative information systems in the two countries.

Through these prints we can trace the development of an urban culture based on print which was not directly derived from the world of 'high' culture, and of the impact of various technological and commercial changes on the cultural universe inhabited by the rural and the urban poor.

Cheap prints should not automatically be taken to have had an exclusively poor audience. Art historians can very often know who a picture was painted for, who it was first bought by, and what a critic thought of it. Not so with cheap prints. Here we find ourselves forced to argue from the structure and evolution of a form to the structure and evolution of a market and an audience. There is some evidence to support this argument, and we can thus consider how the form and its likely audience formed part of the evolving tangle that historians have come to call popular culture.

Cheap prints permit us to see the sorts of things that could be pictured in certain cultural milieux, and the sorts of things that were absent from them. One can, for example, see in French popular imagery of the Revolutionary period the failure of this form to articulate images of political events and processes which were being successfully turned into images for a slightly richer, rather more metropolitan public.

Cheap prints allow us to examine some of the ways in which 'high' cultural forms, such as ideas about the law and the Divinity, or the conventions of pictorial perspective, trickled down into less privileged milieux, and how they were adapted in these new milieux and forms to meet new needs. Besides this many of them provide us with striking or beautiful images, which make this aspect of the study of popular culture in the modernising world not only constantly intriguing, but often unexpectedly pleasurable.

FURTHER READING

Antal, F., *Florentine Painting and its Social Background* (London, 1948); Baxandall, M., *Painting and Experience in Fifteenth-Century Italy: A Primer in the Social History of Pictorial Style* (Oxford, 1972); *Patterns of Invention: On the Historical Explanation of Pictures* (New Haven and London, 1985); Berger, J., *Ways of Seeing* (London, 1972); Borzello, F. and Rees, A. (eds), *The New Art History* (London, 1986); Clark, T. J., *The Absolute Bourgeois: Artists and Politics in France 1848–51* and *The Image of the People: Gustave Courbet and the 1848 Revolution* (London, 1973, p/back, 1981); *The Painting of Modern Life* (London, 1985); Crow, T. E., *Painters and Public Life in Eighteenth-Century Paris* (New Haven and London, 1985); Crowe, J. A. and Cavalcaselle, G. B., *Titian: His Life and Times* (London, 1977); Gombrich, E., *Art and Illusion* (Oxford, 1960); Gretton, T., *Murders and Moralities: English Catchpenny Prints 1800–1860* (London, 1980); Hadjinicolaou, N., *Art History and Class Struggle* (trans. Asmal, L.) (London, 1973); Haskell, F., *Patrons and Painters: Study in the Relations between Italian Art and Society in the Age of the Baroque* (New Haven and London, 1980); Ivins, W., *Prints and Visual Communications* (Cambridge, Mass., 1953); James, L., *Print and the People 1819–1851* (London, 1976); Panofsky, E., *The Life and Art of Albrecht Dürer* (Princeton, 1955); Podro, M., *The Critical Historians of Art* (New Haven and London, 1982); Seznec, J., *The Survival of the Pagan Gods* (trans. Barbara F. Sessions) (New York, 1961); Shepherd, L., *The History of Street Literature* (Newton Abbot, 1973); Vasari, G., *Le Vite de' Piu Eccellenti Pittori, Scultori et Architettori* (Florence, 1568), selection in Eng. trans., *Lives of the Artists* (Harmondsworth, 1965); Wind, E., *Pagan Mysteries in the Renaissance* (London, 1958, Harmondsworth, 1967); *French Popular Imagery: Five Centuries of Prints* (Arts Council exhibition catalogue, 1974).

THE CONTRIBUTORS

Tom Gretton is Lecturer in History of Art at University College, London, and author of *Murders and Moralities: English Catchpenny Prints 1800–1860* (London, 1980).

Charles Hope is Lecturer in Renaissance Studies at the Warburg Institute, University of London, and author of *Titian* (London, 1980).

John House is Lecturer in History of Art at the Courtauld Institute, University of London, and co-author of *Renoir*, exhibition catalogue, Hayward Gallery, London, 1985.

Alex Potts is Principal Lecturer in the History of Art at Camberwell School of Arts and Crafts and author of *Wincklemann's History of the Art of Antiquity* (forthcoming).

9. WHAT IS
INTELLECTUAL
HISTORY . . . ?

The distillation of the 'spirit of the age'? The history of
abstract conceptions of intellectuals? The history of
philosophy? Or the philosophy of history? The history of
political ideas? What is intellectual history?

Stefan Collini

The labels of all the various branches of history are flags of
convenience not names of essences, and the real question concerns
the distinctiveness and validity of their claims to occupy a separate
room in Clio's spacious house. For intellectual history most certainly
is a part of history, part of the attempt to understand past human
experience.

Its role in the division of labour is the understanding of those
ideas, thoughts, arguments, beliefs, assumptions, attitudes and
preoccupations that together made up the intellectual or reflective
life of previous societies. This intellectual life was, of course,
continuous with, and not rigidly separable from, the political life,
the economic life, and so on, of the same societies, but in practice a
rough and ready distinction is intuitively recognisable: where the
economic historian may, for example, want to know about the kinds
of crops grown on the lands of medieval monasteries, the intellectual historian will characteristically be more interested in the ideas to
be seen at work in the monastic chronicles or in the theological basis
of ideals of the contemplative life.

Similarly, it is true that all historians are in practice interpreters of
texts, whether they be private letters, government records, parish
registers, sales lists, or whatever. But for most kinds of historians
these texts are only the necessary means to understanding something other than the texts themselves, such as a political action or a
demographic trend, whereas for the intellectual historian a full
understanding of his chosen texts is itself the aim of his enquiries.
For this reason, intellectual history is particularly prone to draw on
the contributions of those other disciplines that are habitually
concerned with interpreting texts for purposes of their own, such as
the trained sensibilities of the literary critic, alert to all forms of

affective and non-literal writing, or the analytical skills of the philosopher, probing the reasoning that ostensibly connects premisses and conclusions. Furthermore, the boundaries with adjacent subdisciplines are necessarily shifting and indistinct: the history of art and the history of science both claim a certain autonomy, partly just because they require specialised technical skills, but both can also be seen as part of a wider intellectual history, as is evident when one considers, for example, the common stock of knowledge about cosmological beliefs or moral ideals of a period upon which both may need to draw.

Like all historians, the intellectual historian is a consumer rather than a producer of 'methods'; similarly he can claim no type of evidence that is peculiarly and exclusively his. His distinctiveness lies in *which* aspect of the past he is trying to illuminate, not in having exclusive possession of either a corpus of evidence or a body of techniques.

That being said, it does seem that the label 'intellectual historian' attracts a disproportionate share of misunderstanding, and the term 'the history of ideas' is sometimes used as a less eyebrow- or hair-raising alternative. But there is a double hazard in this. First, the emphasis on the 'history of *ideas*' may suggest that we are dealing with autonomous abstractions which, in their self-propelled journeyings through time, happened only accidentally and temporarily to find anchorage in particular human minds, a suggestion encouraged by the comparable German tradition of *Geistesgeschichte* or *Ideengeschichte* which drew upon the history of philosophy in general and Hegel in particular. By contrast, the term 'intellectual history' indicates that the focus is on an aspect of human activity, in the same way as the terms 'economic history' or 'political history' do.

Secondly, 'the history of ideas' was the label chosen in the 1920s and 1930s by the American philosopher-turned-historian, A. O. Lovejoy, to designate his own idiosyncratic approach to the life of the past, an approach which consisted essentially of isolating the universal 'unit-ideas' out of which, he claimed, all more complex doctrines and theories were composed. Through his many pupils and his founding in 1940 of the *Journal of the History of Ideas*, Lovejoy's approach dominated the field in American universities for at least a generation, leading to the compilation of immensely thorough but essentially arid lists of the sightings of particular 'unit-ideas'. Lovejoy's own practice was, as is so often the case, better either than his preaching or than the imitative practice of his disciples, and his most famous work, *The Great Chain of Being* (1936), remains an extremely impressive *tour de force*. Though his influence has fallen away in recent decades (and the journal he founded has become less mechanical and sectarian in its approach), the term 'the history of ideas' is, at least in the United States, still sufficiently often identified with his work as to cause misunderstanding all of its own.

Purely terminological matters aside, it is still the case that much of the suspicion or hostility directed at intellectual history arises out of misconceptions about what it involves, and at this point the most profitable way to respond to our initial question may be to confront these misconceptions directly.

The first alleges that intellectual history is the history of something that never really *mattered*. The long dominance of the historical profession by political historians bred a kind of philistinism, an unspoken belief that power and its exercise was what 'mattered' (a term which invited but rarely received any close critical scrutiny). This prejudice was reinforced, especially where the spirit of Namier was received at all hospitably, by the assertion that political action was never really the outcome of principles or ideas, which were, in the gruff demotic of the land-owning classes, as mimicked by Namier, 'mere flapdoodle'. The legacy of this prejudice is still discernible in the tendency to require ideas to have 'influenced' the political class before they can be deemed worthy of historical attention, as if there were some reason why the history of art or of science, of philosophy or of literature, were somehow of less interest and significance than the history of parties or parliaments.

Perhaps in recent years the mirror-image of this philistinism has become more common in the form of the claim that ideas of any degree of systematic expression or sophistication do not matter because they were, by definition, only held by a minority. As an objection, there is none more worthy of extended rebuttal than its parent prejudice (against which it is in full Oedipal revolt). Needless to say – at least, it ought to be needless to say it – much that legitimately interests us in history was the work of minorities (not always of the same type, be it noted), and, if I may repeat an adaptation of a famous line of E. P. Thompson's that I have used elsewhere, it is not only the poor and inarticulate who may stand in need of being rescued from the enormous condescension of posterity.

The second misconception is that intellectual history is inherently 'idealist', where that term is used pejoratively to signify the belief that ideas develop by a logic of their own, without reference to other human activities, or to what is loosely called their 'social context'. There was possibly some truth to this as a criticism of some of the work written a couple of generations ago, particularly that deriving from the largely German-influenced history of philosophy; but it is simply false as a description of what intellectual history must be like. In the search for fuller understanding, the intellectual historian may well inquire into, say, the economic conditions of certain kinds of authorship, such as aristocratic patronage or serialisation in popular periodicals, just as the economic historian may have to attend to, say, the role of scientific inventions or beliefs about the legitimacy of profit.

There is no reason, however, to accord any explanatory priority to such matters. If, for example, the historian is seeking a deeper insight into the writings of David Hume, it will profit him very little to know more about the economic circumstances of other younger sons of minor Scottish land-owners in the early eighteenth century, whereas his interpretation will gain immensely from knowing something about the writings of a French soldier, an English doctor and an Irish bishop during the previous hundred years (Descartes, Locke, and Berkeley respectively). And, in general, the 'social context' of intellectual activity turns out to have a limited explanatory role in practice, however enthusiastically one may endorse a 'sociological' approach in principle, and this is particularly true the more one grapples with the details of any particular episode in the intellectual life of the past: however much we may know about the social position of the man of letters in Victorian England, we shall have to look to a quite different kind of evidence to achieve a sensitive understanding of the critical controversies between Matthew Arnold and Fitzjames Stephen.

The third misconception, one of more interest and subtlety than the previous two, is that intellectual history is nothing more than the history of the various disciplines of intellectual enquiry. This obviously has some plausibility for the most recent periods, where one could imagine an intellectual history of the nineteenth century being constructed by stringing together the history of science, the history of political economy, the history of philosophy, the history of the novel, and so on. But, other difficulties aside, this would only be to provide the raw materials for an intellectual history of the period, and might, moreover, present them so much with an eye to subsequent developments in each of these fields as to get in the way of a properly historical understanding of what it meant to think such thoughts at the time.

And what about the 'spaces' between these particular activities, or those bits of the intellectual life of the past that have not happened to mutate into labels over the doors of late-twentieth-century university departments? Who, for that matter, has a proprietary right to write the histories of these subjects? An economist *may* be able to reconstruct the proto-economic thought of the seventeenth century in a way that is not distorted by twentieth-century professional concerns, but should we really look to a professor of medicine for an informed and historically sensitive account of the theory of the four humours? And what about those parts of past thought that have *not* issued in modern academic disciplines: are we really to leave the history of astrology, so influential on so many of the most sophisticated minds of the Renaissance, to be written by gypsy ladies in tents? The intellectual historian obviously cannot be confined by such subject-divisions, and insofar as he takes any cognisance of them it may well be above all to explain the mixture of logic and accident that has led to their assuming their present form.

The fourth misconception which it is worth addressing here is that intellectual history must have a method or theory or set of concepts that is distinctively its own. Indeed, in these methodology-conscious and discipline-proliferating days the very fact that I am identifying it as a practicably separable and intellectually justifiable activity may give the impression that I am advocating a tight theoretical programme of how it should be done. But this is not so. Mannheim's *Wissensociologie*, Lovejoy's history of 'unit ideas', the *Annales* school's *Histoire des Mentalités*, Foucault's *Archéologie du Savoir* – each has proposed its own special vocabulary and its own theory of the only possible way to understand the thoughts of the past and each has been found wanting. Good work has certainly been done under the aegis of these different theories, and they have helped inoculate historians against their occupational disease of mindless empiricism. But, as always, the merits of the history written depends on qualities which no theory can adequately prescribe, and it can be argued that the richness of characterisation and fineness of discrimination needed to do justice to the expression of human consciousness, past or present, are unlikely to be encapsulated in the rigid conceptual boxes of some purpose-built vocabulary.

'By their fruits ye shall know them.' In the end, it is the very tangible merits or recent works in this field that constitute the most persuasive argument for recognising intellectual history's title to a room in Clio's house, and they suggest that the throng in the attic study is no less brilliant than that in the political historian's drawing-room, that it is discussing matters no less vital than those treated in the basement kitchen of the economic historians, and that it is dealing with human passions no less profound than those engaged in the back-bedroom of the social historians.

Quentin Skinner

The study of the great religious and philosophical systems of the past; the study of ordinary people's beliefs about heaven and earth, past and future, metaphysics and science; the examination of our ancestors' attitudes towards youth and age, war and peace, love and hate, cabbages and kings; the uncovering of their prejudices about what one ought to eat, how one ought to dress, whom one ought to admire; the analysis of their assumptions about health and illness, good and evil, morals and politics, birth, copulation and death – all these and a vast range of kindred topics fall within the capacious orbit of intellectual history. For they are all instances of the general subject-matter that preoccupies intellectual historians above all: the study of past thoughts.

Given the almost bewildering variety of topics that intellectual historians have considered, it is hardly surprising to find that the subject has been practised in a correspondingly wide range of intellectual styles. I shall confine myself to examining a number of approaches commonly adopted by historians of social and political theory, this being the corner of the discipline in which I am mainly interested myself.

Some choose to focus their attention on the very general concepts or 'unit ideas' which have appeared and reappeared throughout our history in many different theories of social and political life. As a result, they have provided us with histories of such concepts as liberty, equality, justice, progress, tyranny and the other key terms we use to construct and appraise our social and political world. Of late, however, this kind of history of ideas has been much criticised. One worry has been that it tends to leave us with a history almost bereft of recognisable agents, a history in which we find Reason itself overcoming Custom, Progress confronting the Chain of Being, and so forth. But the main doubt about the method has been that, in focusing on ideas rather than their uses in argument, it has seemed insensitive to the strongly contrasting ways in which a given concept can be put to work by different writers in different historical periods.

Another method, currently far more popular with historians of social and political theory, consists of singling out those texts which have been most influential in shaping our western political tradition and offering as careful as possible an account of how they are put together. This too has given rise to a distinguished literature, including many classic monographs on such major figures as Plato and Aristotle, Hobbes and Locke, Rousseau, Hegel, Marx and their contemporary followers.

At the same time, however, this approach has also fallen under suspicion in recent years. Critics have pointed out that if we wish, say, to understand a work such as Hobbes's *Leviathan*, it cannot be enough to furnish an analysis of the propositions and arguments contained in the text. We also need to be able to grasp what Hobbes was *doing* in presenting just those propositions and arguments. We need to be able, that is, to recognise how far he may have been accepting and reiterating accepted commonplaces, or perhaps rephrasing and reworking them, or perhaps criticising and repudiating them altogether in order to attain a new perspective on a familiar theme. But we obviously cannot hope to gain such a sense of the identity of a text, and of its author's basic purposes in writing it, if we confine ourselves simply to analysing the contents of the text itself.

The danger with both the approaches I have singled out is obviously anachronism. Neither seems capable of recovering the precise historical identity of a given text. For neither seems sufficiently interested in the deep truth that concepts must not be viewed simply as propositions with meanings attached to them; they must also be thought of as weapons (Heidegger's suggestion) or as tools (Wittgenstein's term). It follows that to understand a particular concept and the text in which it occurs, we not only need to recognise the meanings of the terms used to express it; we also need to know who is wielding the concept in question, and with what argumentative purposes in mind.

What kind of intellectual history can hope to do justice to this insight? Among those whose particular interest lies in the study of social and political ideas, a new and challenging answer has been emerging over the past two decades. The suggestion has been that we need to focus not on texts or unit ideas, but rather on the entire social and political vocabularies of given historical periods. Beginning in this way, it is claimed, we may eventually be able to fit the major texts into their appropriate intellectual contexts, pointing to the fields of meaning out of which they arose, and to which they in turn contributed.

By now it is possible to point to a number of distinguished practitioners of this approach. John Dunn's classic monograph, *The Political Thought of John Locke*, shows how far the familiar understanding of Locke's politics as 'liberal' derives from an anachronistic misreading, failing as it does to take account of the context of Calvinist natural theology which alone makes sense of Locke's *Two Treatises*. Donald Winch in *Adam Smith's Politics* similarly shows how much we misunderstand *The Wealth of Nations* if we treat it simply as a 'contribution' to classical economics, while ignoring the context of moral theory to which it was addressed. A further example is the book that Winch recently wrote with John Burrow and Stefan Collini, *That Noble Science of Politics*. This provides us with a fascinating survey of what the idea of political science meant to those who first conceived of the discipline, a survey completely free of the gross anachronisms that generally mark the history of the social sciences.

A similar approach to intellectual history has been emerging of recent years in France, especially under the impetus of Michel Foucault's sensational announcement of 'the death of the author' and his allied demand for a study of 'discourses'. Finally, no survey of what has been called 'the new history of political thought' can ignore the work of J. G. A. Pocock. In a series of influential pronouncements about method, Pocock has called on historians of political ideas to concentrate not on texts or traditions of thought, but rather on what he calls the study of political 'languages'. At the same time, he has brilliantly practised what he has preached. His major work, *The Machiavellian Moment*, has uncovered the elements of a Machiavellian moralism at the heart of the republican political tradition in the United States, and has thereby pointed to a need to rewrite the entire history of American liberal thought.

I have ended, inevitably, not just by saying what I think intellectual history is, but how I think it ought to be practised. Certainly I think that, if the history of ideas is to have a genuinely historical character, the new approach I have mentioned is the one that most deserves to be followed up.

David A. Hollinger

'Intellectual history' is a convenient label for a number of scholarly activities being carried out by persons trained in a number of disciplines of which history is only one. Especially have philosophy, literary criticism, and politics produced exemplary intellectual historians. This is true in the United States as well as in Britain and on the Continent, although professional historians in America have dealt with intellectual history rather differently than have their counterparts across the Atlantic. American academia has long recognised as a subdiscipline of history itself studies of the sort that most British and European scholars still tend to see as 'history of literature' or 'history of philosophy'. But from this American perspective, what *is* 'intellectual history'?

It is, quite simply, the history of what intellectuals have said about issues that historians regard as important. This definition captures the commonsense image that generally comes to mind when someone mentions 'intellectual history'. Who are the 'intellectuals'? Although there exists a recondite literature on the qualities that render one a true intellectual (is he or she sufficiently *critical? knowledgeable? serious? smart?*), we need not put quite so fine a point on it. An 'intellectual' for my purpose here is one who, whatever else he or she may have done in life, made *thinking* enough of an enterprise to get himself or herself into the tracings that remain of that particular human activity as carried out during his or her own time.

'Thinking' is an extremely broad category of action, comparable to the activities – 'social living'? the exercise of 'power'? – that define social and political history. The intellect, like society and politics, is subject to specific constructions that render our sub-disciplines in practice less comprehensive than they are in theory. In the case of intellectual history, two frequently overlapping constructions of the field's ideal subject matter are supported by large professional constituencies. The vocabulary by which historians distinguish between these two constructions is currently in flux, but something of the distinction is conveyed by several classical, if sometimes misleading dichotomies: élite-mass, learned-popular, ideas-feelings, analytic-symbolic, and rational-religious.

The first construction takes for its primary datum the discursive arguments of scientists, philosophers, critics, preachers, scholars, and others who self-consciously addressed 'intellectual issues'. Early classics of this genre of history include Leslie Stephen's *History of English Thought in the Eighteenth Century* (2 volumes, 1876) and J. T. Merz's *A History of European Thought in the Nineteenth Century* (4 volumes, 1904–1912). It was in this tradition that the professional field of 'intellectual history' took form in the United States during the 1930s and 1940s under the influence of Vernon Louis Parrington, Merle Curti, and above all Perry Miller, whose *The New England Mind* (2 volumes, 1939–1953) has been invoked more than any other single work of American scholarship to indicate what is meant by 'intellectual history'.

The second construction focuses on the myths, symbols, and languages drawn upon by large populations for the purposes of making sense of life or of given aspects of it. Inspired in part by cultural anthropology and literary criticism, this genre of intellectual history is even broader than the first. Henry Nash Smith's *Virgin Land: The American West in Symbol and Myth* (1950) was long its most discussed American exemplar. Smith and his followers focused primarily on literary texts and the popular arts, but in more recent years, partly in response to the studies of *mentalité* carried out by French historians, the genre has been enlarged to embrace the study of rituals and other non-discursive indicators of meaning. In terms of the definition I offered above, this genre of intellectual history has expanded traditional understandings of what counts as an 'issue', what is included in the realm of the 'said', what historical artefacts are to be interpreted as 'tracings' of the activity of thought, and hence who is an 'intellectual'. William J. Bouwsma has characterised this genre's relation to the old in terms of a transition in fashion 'from the history of ideas to the history of meaning'. The two genres overlap increasingly as students of 'popular culture' seek to confront the dynamic element, the actual thinking, done by their subjects, and as students of 'intellectual élites' seek to confront the relatively static languages within which their subjects perform analytic acts of mind, whilst the accommodation of the 'history of ideas' to the newer scholarship that prefers to speak of 'structures of meaning' has been decisively advanced in the United States by the influence of the late Michel Foucault.

J. G. A. Pocock

What is intellectual history? You may well ask, but I am not sure I can tell you.

Whatever 'intellectual history' is, and whatever 'the history of ideas' may be, I am not engaged in doing either of them.

The two terms appear in fact to mean about the same thing: a species of metahistory or theory of history, an enquiry into the nature of history based on various theories about how intellect or 'ideas' find a place in it, with the result that what you usually get is the philosophy of history or the history of philosophy. I do not mean to speak disrespectfully of this pursuit. It was developed by Germans in the nineteenth century, and recently there have been the inevitable French – Michel Foucault and Jacques Derrida – who set out to destroy the enterprise altogether and succeeded in perpetuating it instead. All these have been profound, subtle, and sensitive minds, but they live several crystalline spheres further out than I do. I do not share their concerns; I am not sure I can state what these are; and I have not succeeded in learning very much from them which illuminates what I think I am doing. Nevertheless, I find myself classified as 'an intellectual historian' or 'an historian of ideas', and asked to answer questions like this one. The best I can do is describe my own practice, in the hope that it will prove informative.

I think I am a historian of a certain kind of intellectual activity, which used to be and sometimes still is called 'the history of political thought' – though I would like to find a replacement for the last word, not because thought wasn't going on, but because it doesn't adequately characterise the activity whose history I aim to write. I would like to use instead the word 'discourse' – meaning 'speech', 'literature' and public utterance in general, involving an element of theory and carried on in a variety of contexts with which it can be connected in a variety of ways. The advantage of this approach is that it enables one to write the history of an intellectual activity as a history of actions performed by human beings in a variety of circumstances; actions which have affected other human beings, and have affected the circumstances in which they were performed (if only by making it possible to talk and argue about these circumstances).

Human beings inhabiting political societies find themselves first surrounded by political institutions and conventions, second performing political actions and third engaging in political practices. In the course of doing so they speak, write, print, appear on television, and so on; they employ words and other sign systems; and language is not just a means of talking about these actions and institutions, but a means of performing the actions and operating the institutions. And vice versa: when you speak (or write or print) you not merely perform an action, but talk about the action you are performing. (J. L. Austin, *How To Do Things With Words*, Oxford University Press, 1962.)

Political societies generate a constant flow of language and discourse, in which actions are both performed and discussed. Language furnishes not only the practice of politics, but also its theory. The language-using agents not only utter, but argue; they reply in speech to one another's speech acts, challenge one another's use of words and demand clarification of one another's meanings. As a result there arises what is known as second-order language or theory; speech about speech, in which language is used not only to practise politics and to discuss the practice of politics, but to discuss the ways in which language itself is used to do both these things. This is a point of departure at which one can take off from politics to arrive at 'intellectual history' and 'the history of ideas' in the high and far-off senses mentioned earlier. It is also the point at which the historian finds that a great deal of the discussion in the history of politics has been discussion of how language is and ought to be used in the contexts furnished by particular political societies. And it is the point at which one moves from political theory – the discussion of how political systems work and how words work in them – to political philosophy: the discussion of how statements made in political societies can have any meaning, and of how the political societies themselves look in the light of the theories of meaning and truth thus arrived at. The historian of political discourse does not have to be a historian of political philosophy, but he/she will notice that philosophy is one of the activities generated by political discourse.

And that is really all there is to it; at least, to what I claim to be doing. People develop political languages and say things in them; saying things leads them in various directions. I do not claim to be a hard-headed practical man with no need of theory; for one thing, I am writing the history of an activity which includes the generation of theory, and for another I need some theory to explain what my practice is. I have tried to supply one in the introduction to *Virtue*,

Commerce and History (Cambridge University Press, 1985). I am reasonably content with what I am doing, but like Odysseus I have to sail between Charybdis and Scylla. Charybdis, the all-engulfing whirlpool, stands for the philosphers of history who complain because I have no general theory of history; Scylla the monster with many barking heads, stands for the bullying social realists who think they already know what social reality is, assume that it is more or less misrepresented in the languages used in society, and nevertheless demand that language shall be connected with it at every possible point. I can disagree with the former and remain on good terms with them; the latter are impossible because I am already doing what they ask for and they won't see it.

Michael Hunter

What *is* intellectual history? The best approach is to begin with what might be considered the inner sanctum of the subject, and to work outwards from there.

At least as it has been habitually practised, the focus of intellectual history is the study of the 'high' ideas of past periods, the views of intellectuals who participated in the learned culture of their time, writers who – in the sixteenth and seventeenth centuries – often wrote their books in the international learned language of Latin. Attention has been paid both to the philosophical and other theoretical ideas of an era and to its erudition – whether in history, science or even a subject like demonology – and the characteristic techniques deployed include the exact analysis of authors' arguments and methods, the assessment of their background, sources and originality, and hence the reconstruction of the process of intellectual development at the time.

Such studies frequently focus on specific authors, if only as a means of building up a broader picture, and the writers typically selected for such analysis are thinkers and scholars singled out for the quality of their intellect rather than for their literary gifts or the size of their readership. Classic examples would include Anthony Grafton's recent study of the great historian and chronologer, Joseph Scaliger (*Joseph Scaliger: A Study in the History of Classical Scholarship*, 1983), which resurrects a whole world of complex ideas which would otherwise have remained buried in voluminous, unread tomes. Equally characteristic is Richard H. Popkin's *History of Scepticism from Erasmus to Descartes*, originally published in 1960 (retitled *A History of Scepticism from Erasmus to Spinoza*, 1980), or D. P. Walker's learned study of the magical ideas of thinkers ranging from Cornelius Agrippa to Francis Bacon in *Spiritual and Demonic*

Magic from Ficino to Campanella (1958).

But, if this is the area in which the subject-matter of intellectual history is most clearly defined, its boundaries are far from precise, as high ideas merge into middle-brow ones, and as one moves from thinkers in the vanguard of contemporary thought to others who purveyed less original notions. After all, intellectual history has a less forbidding synonym in the form of 'the history of ideas', and this is a term which is in many ways preferable, implying as it does a broader range of subject-matter of which the most abstruse ideas form only a part.

The ideas of a mediocre intellect may teach us as much about contemporary thought as those of the most original: my own study, *John Aubrey and the Realm of Learning* (1975), might be placed in this category, since Aubrey is interesting as much for the commonplace ideas to which he gave memorable expression as for his originality on some of the topics he studied. In addition, there is an important place for the study of the shared ideas of a larger historical group in the form of the literate class as a whole. Here one thinks of E. M. W. Tillyard's famous essay, *The Elizabethan World Picture* (1943), as exemplifying a whole genre which has sought to reconstruct the commonly accepted ideas of a period, often in an attempt to make sense of assumptions underlying contemporary literature.

The work of Keith Thomas, and perhaps particularly his recent study of *Man and the Natural World* (1983), falls into a comparable category, chronicling widely held ideas rather then erudite ones, but ideas which, it can be argued, were frequently more significant than those of ivory-towered intellectuals. Here, different techniques may come into play, particularly the juxtaposition of statements by a range of interlocutors to give a sense of shared opinions of the time, a technique which Keith Thomas' writings exemplify well.

What is the boundary of such studies? In theory there is none, but in practice limitations are imposed by the availability of source materials. The history of ideas, or intellectual history, depends on a sufficient body of ideas being available to be susceptible to serious analysis, and this generally means a limitation to the ideas of the literate and to the habitually articulate. This may be illustrated by occasional exceptions to the rule, as with the ideas of the Friuli miller, Menocchio, preserved through the attentions of the Inquisition: these provided the materials for a study by Carlo Ginzburg in *The Cheese and the Worms* (English translation, 1980), in which many of the skills of the intellectual historian are deployed. The proliferation of radical ideas during and after the English Civil War is a comparable instance, reflected by a plethora of studies of which perhaps the most notable is Christopher Hill's *The World Turned Upside Down* (1972).

Indeed, if anything there is currently a danger of such ideas receiving disproportionate attention while those of the learned are fashionably disdained. But this would be a mistake. In fact, a proper understanding of the thought of any period will depend on knowing about all ideas that were current, from the popular to the erudite. Moreover the spectrum of ideas thus laid out should not be taken for granted but should be the subject of investigation in itself. The interconnection of ideas among different cultural strata in society cries out for attention: a study which does justice to that will have the best claims to be called the true intellectual history of its chosen period.

FURTHER READING

Berlin, I., *Against the Current: Essays in the History of Ideas* (London, 1979); Boucher, D., *Texts and Contexts: Revisionist Methods for Studying the History of Ideas* (Dordrecht, 1985); Burrow, J. W., *A Liberal Descent: Victorian Historiography and the English Past* (Cambridge, 1981); Burrow, J. W., Collini, S. and Winch, D., *That Noble Science of Politics: a study in Nineteenth-Century Intellectual History* (Cambridge, 1984); Condred, C., *The Status and Appraisal of Classical Texts* (Princeton, 1985); Foucault, M., *The Archaeology of Knowledge* (London, 1972); Gay, P., *The Enlightenment: An Interpretation* (two vols) (New York, 1966, 1970); Gilbert, F., *Machiavelli and Guicciardini: Politics and Historiography in Sixteenth-Century Florence* (Princeton, 1965); Gunn, J. A., *Beyond Liberty and Property: the Process of Self-Recognition in Eighteenth-Century Political Thought* (Kingston and Montreal, 1983); Higham, J., *Writing American History* (Bloomington, Indiana, 1970); King, P. (ed.), *The History of Ideas* (Beckenham, 1983); Kuhn, T. S., *The Structure of Scientific Revolutions* (Chicago, 1962); La Capra, D. and Kaplan, S. L. (eds), *Modern European Intellectual History* (Cornell, 1982); Lovejoy, A. O., *The Great Chain of Being: the History of an Idea* (Cambridge, Mass., 1936); Skinner, Q., *Studies in Early Modern Intellectual History* (Cambridge, forthcoming); Thomas, K., *Religion and the Decline of Magic* (London, 1971), *Man and the Natural World* (London, 1983); Wallace, J. M., *Destiny his Choice: the Loyalism of Andrew Marvell* (Cambridge, 1986).

THE CONTRIBUTORS

Stefan Collini is Reader in Intellectual History at the University of Sussex and author of *Liberalism and Sociology: L. T. Hobhouse and Political Argument in England, 1880–1914* (Cambridge, 1983), and (with J. W. Burrow and D. Winch) *That Noble Science of Politics: a Study in Nineteenth-Century Intellectual History* (Cambridge, 1983).

David A. Hollinger is Professor of History at the University of Michigan and author of *In the American Province: Studies in the History and Historiography of Ideas* (Indiana, 1985).

Michael Hunter is Reader in History at Birkbeck College, University of London, and author of *Science and Society in Restoration England* (Cambridge, 1981).

J. G. A. Pocock is Professor of History at Johns Hopkins University, Baltimore, and author of *Virtue, Commerce and History* (Cambridge, 1985).

Quentin Skinner is Professor of Political Science at the University of Cambridge and author of *Machiavelli* (Oxford, 1981).

10. WHAT IS
THE HISTORY OF
POPULAR CULTURE?

*Another note towards a definition of culture? The history of
leisure? True insights into the 'mind set' of an age? The
study of anecdotalism and ephemera collecting? The history
of the excluded? The history of modes of communication and
perception? The study of the opium of the people? What is
the history of popular culture?*

Asa Briggs

It is easier to participate in, to enjoy, to deplore, or to explore
popular culture than it is to define it. This is not simply because
there are difficulties in relating *popular* culture to culture (and sub-
cultures) or to *folk* culture – some of these difficulties are of the
historian's making, particularly the Marxist historian's – but because of the inherent difficulties in defining 'culture' itself. It was
not because of his particular political or cultural stance that T. S.
Eliot chose to collect 'notes towards a definition of culture' rather
than to offer a definition of his own.

I seldom use the term 'popular culture' myself, although I am
deeply interested in its history and in the various meanings attached
to it. The language of 'mass culture' has appealed to me even less,
although I have tried to trace its history too. I have found some of the
detailed American studies of selected aspects of it extremely
stimulating, particularly those with a sense of fun. I like the attempt
too to evaluate as well as to analyse and interpret. This has its origins
in literature rather than in social studies. Story-telling counts.

Leaving on one side the terms, the field of popular culture has
attracted me for a number of reasons. I approached it first through
the history of broadcasting, going on to explore the neglected
history of entertainment in a pre-broadcasting age. I was interested
from the start not only in the institutions which acted as providers,
but in the 'output'. The BBC's concern with 'popular culture' was
slow to develop under Reith and after him never complete, but it
was revealing at every stage in its history to compare both the
institutional shell of the BBC and its programming with those of
American media agencies, including the cinema, and I was for-

120

tunate enough to spend nine interesting years at an interesting time as Governor of the British Film Institute.

BBC output by itself was wide enough to draw me into a study of the history of almost every facet of twentieth-century culture, including sport and popular music, subjects the history of which had interested me even before I turned to broadcasting. Indeed, I was completing a kind of circle in my own research when I studied them in a broadcasting context. It was not so much research, however, that encouraged re-evaluation and re-orientation but the input from current popular culture itself, sometimes exciting, often disturbing. Inevitably I became concerned, too, with the history of leisure and the different attitudes towards it at different times.

Charting went with exploration, and I felt and still feel that the problems of periodisation are as interesting as those of structures. The two are in fact, directly related. I pushed my own interests back before the industrial revolution and encouraged researchers to do the same. The cultural 'side' of the industrial revolution, not least the popular cultures of steam technology, began to interest me more than the economic 'side', although I have always been sceptical about cultural studies which leave the economics out.

It is on the basis of specific studies that I have developed a general sense of what the history of popular culture is and should be. Like the exploration of culture itself, it must be concerned with content as well as context, with work as well as play, with place as well as time, with religion as well as technology, with communication as well as with expression, with provision and participation as well as performance, with the visual and the musical as well as the verbal.

All these figure in my own notes towards a definition. Present work in progress includes work on publishing history (which links the history of popular culture with education), on nineteenth-century music (which links the history of popular culture with the history of 'high culture') and on Victorian artefacts (including photographs). The last of these topics has received less attention than the first two. The concept of 'material culture' certainly brings in both the economics and the psychology, not to speak of many of the fashionable ideological preoccupations of recent years. The interdisciplinary nature of all studies of popular culture is obvious. That to me is one of its greatest attractions. Another is that I genuinely like ephemera.

Peter Burke

We may think we know what we mean by the term 'popular culture'. At any rate, we thought we knew what we meant by it when we discovered – in the early 1970s in my case, as in so many others – that it had a history. We decided that we would study the history of the excluded, the dominated, the subordinate groups and classes (whom we refused to call 'the masses') and not only their standard of living but their culture as well. Readers will have noticed that this defines popular culture by what it is not. A positive definition is much more difficult, because the phrase contains two serious ambiguities. Both 'popular' and 'culture' are problematic terms.

Firstly, who are 'the people'? Are they the poor? the powerless? the uneducated? These are negative terms again. And in any case, since all children are brought up by adults, what does 'uneducated' mean? Do different subordinate groups – male and female, young and old, urban and rural – share the same culture and in every society?

Secondly what is culture? My favourite definition is in terms of shared attitudes (meanings, values), expressed (embodied, symbolised) by artefacts and performances. Where high culture has 'art', popular culture has 'artefacts': not only images but tools, houses, the whole man-made environment. Where high culture has 'literature, drama, music', popular culture has 'performances', a term designed to include not only rituals and songs but any kind of talk or action directed to any audience, however small. This is, as definitions go, far from narrow, but I have sometimes been criticised for not widening it still further, to include what is sometimes called 'cultural practice'; the attitudes and values expressed through the act of living one's day-to-day life. It is hard to say what is not 'culture' in this sense of the term. It is also hard to say what is not 'popular', for popular culture is not exclusive like high culture. It is open to all, like the tavern and the marketplace where so many performances traditionally took place. Can we even exclude the social and political élite? They might have a closed culture of their own but this has not always prevented them from taking part in Carnival, singing ballads, reading chap-books. And who today doesn't watch television?

These problems of definition will not go away and cannot be put on one side if one is trying to do research. They are not unique but they are especially acute in the study of any unofficial, informal, open system. Add to this the notorious problem of 'contaminated' sources: the need for historians of all ages before the tape-recorder to study the oral through the written, and popular attitudes through records made by and for élites – and one may be forgiven for sighing occasionally for a well-defined but limited topic, such as the Parliament of 1614.

I don't sigh for very long, actually. These problems are a challenge and historians of popular culture are in the middle of working out new strategies for creeping up on their quarry. One strategy is to concentrate not on 'the people' as such, or even any group within it, but on the interaction between learned and popular cultural traditions. A recent collection of essays (*Understanding Popular Culture*, ed. Steven Kaplan, 1984) makes interaction its central theme, and one of the contributors, Roger Chartier, argues that we should study culture 'as appropriation', searching not for exclusively popular literature (say) as for the different ways in which learned and popular writers and readers used the common material.

I have tried to do this myself in the past and my current research, on modes of communication and perception in different parts of Italy in the sixteenth and seventeenth centuries, begins with media and messages and goes on to discuss who was communicating what to whom via these different channels and codes. The media discussed are the oral (blasphemy, for example), the written (from the love-letter to the 'defamatory libel' posted on one's enemy's door), the language of gesture, of ritual (such as the ritual of the papal coronation), and of images (such as Renaissance portraits). Illness and conspicuous consumption are both viewed, as an anthropologist would view them, that is as forms of communication.

The phrase 'popular culture' may not appear very often in these essays, but the attitudes of ordinary people will not be neglected. The value of a detour is to allow viewpoints inaccessible to those who always take a direct approach.

Dai Smith

Twenty-five years ago 'Popular Culture' was something you popped into a new-fangled holdall bag labelled 'Social History'. Nowadays it threatens to emulate its early protector by evolving into a separate discipline to be studied with the help of such stern interlocutors as the sisters Sociology and Semiolgy. One definition of the history of popular culture lends itself readily to this treatment: it is the description and analysis of the popular tastes, customs, folk beliefs, manners and entertainments within any given social order. In short, it is the culture of most of the people as opposed to the culture organised, thought and transmitted by various élites. Matters become more interesting when we refine the definition to account for the ambiguity that will necessarily accompany the history of popular culture if we insist on its prior and continuing relationship to the material formation of society as a whole.

In his rich compendium, *Peasants Into Frenchmen* (1977), Eugen

Weber demonstrated, with a wealth of example, how the rural population comprehended the particularities of their world through the forms of their own popular culture. He also stressed the tortuous relationship between that 'authentic' way of life and the 'artificial' one being created for them in the wake of the urbanisation and industrialisation of France. An earlier process of change in Britain could be dismissed, by some in the 1930s, as the degeneration of a natural, organic culture and its replacement by a mass one which, in turn, could only be purified by a conscious, culturally-equipped minority. The cultural equipment was, of course, possession of an English literary tradition as selected by F. R. Leavis and fellow scrutineers.

Popular culture was, in this way, equated with the mechanical, the vulgar and the masses. More and more it was synonymous with leisure pursuits and mass circulation newspapers, with soccer and seaside-trips, with tinned peaches and pop music and the passive consumption of what was produced for, rather than by, the people. For both the Left and the Right popular culture was conveniently singled out as the new 'Poppy of the Masses'. This species of reductionism had been applied to the history of religion with equally unenlightening results. Popular culture, too, has been more than just a shadow play of reality. Certainly this is why it has been at the centre of the political and the philosophical debate about the precise order and functioning of life in modern, and now post-modern, society. So its history is as much about interrelationship – say, the rise of universal suffrage and the development of spectator sport – as compartmentalisation of human activity.

This is recognised both by historians whose direct subject is a popular cultural activity like sport itself and by those whose study of grass-roots political change is concerned to see political culture in a surrounding context. Those who read Richard Holt (*Sport and Society in Modern France*, 1981) on why rugby football became a passion in the south-west of France in the late nineteenth-century will find it easy to dovetail his history of sport and *sociabilité* into Tony Judt's (*Socialism in Provence*, 1979) analysis of Provençal communality and socialist politics. And in Britain, David Howell's *British Workers and the Independent Labour Party* (1983) meticulously unites a history of working-class evangelicalism (religious and political) with autodidactic fervour (natural science and philosophy) and a *regional* pace of development. Politics and sport, rugby league and the ILP in west Yorkshire, rugby union and participatory militancy in South Wales are as connected as Eric Hobsbawm once suggested is the social history of the piano and working-class respectability. Commercialism and spontaneity, decision and in-duced desire, the play of liberation and the framework of utility are, in modern times, inseparable.

One difficulty, then, in reconstructing histories of popular culture is that the form could not be linear. The familiar narrative of a political history or a biography could not encompass the cultural experience in action. Recently, T. J. Clark (*The Painting of Modern Life*, 1985) has suggested that the search for new forms by Manet and other Impressionist painters – unfinished, strangely at odds with its own desire to be complete – is a refraction of the contemporary tension (post-1860s) between a collective, proletarian presence and a defining bourgeois identity. The battleground is leisure, suburbia, the spectacle of the city and the choice of sides taken by the *petit bourgeois*. In other words *what* is to be 'popular' in popular culture? All of which sounds to me like the problems traditionally confronted by novelists intent on uncovering the meaning of the signs by which we all live through style and form.

Using our simple definition, the history of popular culture is the sociological translation of the readership tastes for, say, Harold Robbins or J. R. Tolkien from 'fantasy' to 'reality'. There is more mileage in examining the proposition that, say, F. Scott Fitzgerald dissected the mass production of popular culture and showed its sway over a whole society in *The Great Gatsby* (1925). He pulled the diffuse actuality of early twentieth-century America into an essential shape through the agency of a style intent on dramatic relief. This is what Fitzgerald's mentor, Joseph Conrad, meant when he wrote (in 1906), 'Fiction is history, human history, or it is nothing. But it is also more than that . . . being based on the reality of forms and the observation of social phenomenon'.

Most historians would now say 'Amen' to that and recognise that the history of popular culture lies not only in its documented existence but also in its contemporary permeation of all literary genres, whether unmediated except by clichés or unexpectedly revealed in an essential form. And just as traditional history, inescapably bent on excluding popular culture beyond 'local colour', mirrored the techniques of naturalistic fiction, so the latter's replacement by the 'magical realism' of contemporary novelists whose work (Rushdie, Doctorow, Marquez) is suffused with historical sensibility may push historians into a subtler understanding of their own representation of reality on the page. Raymond Carr's comment on Richard Cobb – 'the work of a poet as much of an historian' – might then be seen as no more of an oddity than the coupling of those essential words of modern life – 'popular' and 'culture'. Thereby hang all our histories.

Jeffrey Richards

Cultural history is one of the most complex and demanding branches of historical endeavour. For it requires its practitioners to be equipped not just with the training and tools of the historian but also the analytical skills of the expert in literature and art, the methodological equipment of the sociologist and the conceptual sophistication of the political theorist. The work of the cultural historian, as Raymond Williams argued in his influential book *The Long Revolution* (1975), is to elucidate the meanings and values implicit and explicit in the art, literature, learning, institutions and everyday behaviour within a given society.

Broadly speaking there are two cultures: the high or élite culture and the popular or mass culture. Only in rare instances do the two cultures converge and then but briefly (the 1890s, the Second World War, the 1960s for example). In Britain, Elgar and Kipling are perhaps the last artists of genius to have touched the hearts of ordinary people. For the most part the two cultures are out of synchronisation and sealed off. For the historian concerned with the real spirit of an age, the collective *mentalité*, the popular culture is of greatest value; the high culture often misleads.

For instance, in 1930s Britain the high culture was remorselessly hostile to the public schools and the British Empire, yet these institutions were regularly endorsed by the popular culture and this was an era which saw the landslide election of a largely Conservative national government, joyous royal celebrations like the Silver Jubilee of King George V and a revival of respect and affection for 'Victorianism'. In these circumstances, it is the films of Gracie Fields rather than the poems of W. H. Auden or the novels of Virginia Woolf which give us the best insight into the 'mind-set' of the age.

The succinct statement of the eminent medieval historian Lynn White, 'World-views are better judged by what people do than by what they say', applies particularly to the 'silent majority' of a nation's inhabitants. How they choose to spend their money and in particular on which cultural objects can tell us much about their assumptions and attitudes. For much of this century films have been a central part of popular culture. Cinema-going was the principal leisure activity of a large proportion of the British people from the First World War to the 1950s. A. J. P. Taylor called it 'the essential social habit of the age', and no historian can afford to ignore this vital aspect of everyday life.

In general, the cinema operates in two ways – to reflect and highlight popular attitudes, ideas and preoccupations, and to generate and inculcate views and opinions deemed desirable by film-makers. Film-makers select, in the first case, material which they know will appeal to their audience and in the second, material with which they can manipulate their audience and shape its perceptions. It may well be that a film will aim to do both things at once. The cinema can thus operate as a potent means of social control, transmitting the dominant ideology of a society and creating for it a consensus of support. For films provide images of society, constructed of selected elements and aspects of everyday life, which are organised into a coherent pattern governed by a set of underlying presuppositions. The process of selection confers status on certain issues, institutions and individuals – for instance, the police or the monarchy – which regularly appear in a favourable light.

Popular films (and in particular *genre* films such as crime dramas, horror pictures or westerns, which regularly use the same elements, characters and situations), function as rituals, cementing the beliefs and ideals of society, enforcing social norms and exposing and isolating deviants. It is therefore of major importance to discover who controls the production of films and what attitudes and ideals they are disseminating through them. It is equally important to find out what audiences made of them. For the relationship between films and audience is reciprocal. An audience does not accept passively every message that is put across in a film. In the last resort it is positive audience approval, expressed via the box office, that ensures whether a film succeeds or fails financially. So producers' calculations of what will appeal to their audiences inevitably influence what goes into a film.

Direct propaganda rarely works, as the Nazis discovered in Germany. Their first three feature film exercises in promoting the Nazi party were such box-office disasters that Propaganda Minister Goebbels ordered the direct propaganda to be confined in future to the newsreels and he sought to work more covertly on audiences by inserting propaganda elements into 'straight' entertainment films. Audiences the world over go to the cinema primarily to be entertained not to be instructed. But the content of their celluloid day dreams provides the historian with an entry to their minds.

It is the holistic approach to film history which is the most useful for the historian of popular culture. This requires the analysis of the content and structure of groups of films, the elucidation of box-office trends, the assessment of star personalities and their appeal, the investigation of contemporary reviews and reactions, the reconstruction of the production context (censorship, government policy, company attitudes) and the location of all these elements firmly in their political, social and cultural setting. By doing this, the historian gains insight into the changing social and sexual roles of men and women, the concepts of work and leisure, class and race, peace and war, the determinants of change and continuity in the real world. It is in this way that films in particular and popular culture in general can extend our understanding of recent history.

Stephen Yeo

In the beginning, the words. In this case there is a lot to cut through to get at my own concerns. Popular? Dominant meaning: consumed by many people, most people (but usually not 'the best people'), often by 'the masses'. Example: 'popular music'. Culture? Dominant meanings: either an attribute or possession of 'the best people', or a whole way of life. An example which slides between these alternatives: 'Viennese culture at the turn of the century was the cradle of the modern'. If one wanted to refer to what most Viennese people were like or liked one would have to add: 'Viennese *popular* culture at the turn of the century was . . .'.

These are dense thickets. Raymond Williams' work, from *Culture and Society 1780–1950* (1956) to *Writing in Society* (1984) has been extraordinarily helpful (though not yet used enough) to historians of popular culture. He defines his practice as that of a cultural materialist, intending to transform cultural practice, and thereby a whole society. He shows how crucial cultural relations, conflict and struggle are to what we now think of as 'production' and how crucial relations of production are to what we now think of as 'culture'. History, or the way things (relations) change, is the substance or base in which 'production', 'popular' and 'culture' are represented and will, by socialists, be re-presented.

So, Popular? My meaning here: having to do with what most people like and like doing/making. This is very difficult to get at in the past or the present of a society like ours, unless you regard indices like votes, purchases, or the readership of *The Sun* as adequate. Culture? My meaning here: having to do with *growth*, and with *meanings* One of my favourite books, *The Culture of Vegetables and Flowers from Seeds and Roots*, by Sutton and Sons (Reading, 18th edition, 1930) uses the word appropriately.

My own interest in this field is mainly in *association* as popular culture. I would like to be able to interpret, and to make available for change, how people have associated in this society over the last five hundred years. Forms of association have been intermittent, as in the case of street life or workshop life: they have also been continuous, as in the case of the largest nineteenth-century working-class organisations, the Friendly Societies. Anyone interested in popular culture in Britain would be well advised to look through obvious cultural artefacts such as the novel, to less obvious ones, but central in Britain, such as the meeting, the banner, the rule-book, the newspaper. In her Introduction to *Society and Culture in Early Modern France* (1975), Natalie Zemon Davis put it well:

> It [research] was also a matter of recognizing that forms of associational life and collective behaviour are cultural artefacts, not just items in the history of the Reformation or of political centralization. A journeyman's initiation rite, a village festive organization, an informal gathering of women for a lying-in, of men and women for storytelling, or a street disturbance could be 'read' as fruitfully as a diary, a political tract, a sermon, or a body of laws.

Miners' trade unionism provides a contemporary instance, ripe for 'reading' historically. A formidable cultural achievement by millions of people currently unpopular, it is well-suited to an historical approach interested in 'popular culture'. The achievement of a single Federation in the late nineteenth century, against the grain of regional and economic differences among miners: the invention of forms like block votes within the Union and between it and political allies: festivals: home and family, gender and community culture in their complicated relations with the trade and the Union: the way in which miners have brought the details and the novelties of large-scale democratic practice into critical relations with a culture which has collapsed democracy into 'Parliamentary Democracy As We Know It': the lives of individual miners like Jack Lawson, *A Man's Life* (1932): miners' sense of craft, inheritance and responsibility for places, industries and ways of life (not just 'jobs') . . . all these are material for answering the question, 'what is the history of popular culture?'. To make such connections authentically, I would recommend history-from-within like R. Fynes, *The Miners of Northumberland and Durham* (1873). The connections will never be made without recognising that class conflict, or the struggle between rival clusters of potential, goes on *within* the 'popular' as well as between it and not-popular (élite?, dominant?, high?) culture.

Finally, in the making of history of popular culture, forms of publication and authorship matter, as well as the objects of study. A popular culture without the inverted commas, without dense thickets of class meaning to cut through, will indeed be one in which the objects of study (e.g. miners) become their own subjects. This is why the Barnsley Women Against Pit Closures' book, *Women Against Pit Closures* (1984), the Oxford Miners Support Group's book, *The Miners Strike in Oxford* (1985), and the London Co-op Political Committee's book, *Here We Go! Women's Memories of the 1984/5 Miners Strike* (1985), are such good examples of modern history.

FURTHER READING

Berman, M., *All that is Solid Melts into Air* (London, 1983); Burke, P., *Popular Culture in Early Modern Europe* (London, 1978); Clarke, J., Critcher, C. and Johnson, R., *Working-Class Culture: Studies in History and Theory* (London, 1979); Ginzburg, C., *The Cheese and the Worms: The Cosmos of a Sixteenth-Century Miller* (trans. Tedeschi, J. and A.) (London, 1980); Kaplan, S. (ed.), *Understanding Popular Culture*, (Berlin, 1984); Mackenzie, J. M. (ed.), *Imperialism and Popular Culture*, (Manchester, 1986); Muchembled, R., *Popular Culture and Elite Culture in France 1450–1700* (Baton Rouge, 1985); Reay, B. (ed.), *Popular Culture in Seventeenth-Century England* (Beckenham, 1985); Richards, J. and Aldgate, A., *Best of British: Cinema and Society 1930–1970* (Oxford, 1983); Stedman Jones, G., *Language of Class: Studies in English Working-Class History* (Cambridge, 1983); Storch, R. D. (ed.), *Popular Culture and Custom in Nineteenth-Century England* (Beckenham, 1982); Waites, B., Bennett, T. and Martin, G., *Popular Culture: Past and Present* (Beckenham, 1982); Williams, G., *The Welsh in their History* (Beckenham, 1982); Williams, R., *The Long Revolution* (Harmondsworth, 1975); *Keywords* (London, 1976); *Problems in Materialism and Culture* (London, 1980); *Culture* (London, 1981); Yeo, E. and S. (eds), *Popular Culture and Class Conflict 1590–1914* (Brighton, 1981).

THE CONTRIBUTORS

Asa Briggs is Provost of Worcester College, Oxford, and author of *A Short History of Broadcasting* (Oxford, 1985).

Peter Burke is Fellow of Emmanuel College, Cambridge, and author of *Sociology and History* (London, 1980).

Jeffrey Richards is Senior Lecturer in History at the University of Lancaster, and author of *Age of the Dream Palace. Cinema and Society in Britain 1930–1939* (London, 1984).

Dai Smith is Senior Lecturer in Welsh History at University College, Cardiff, and author of *Wales, Wales?* (London, 1984).

Stephen Yeo is Reader in History at the University of Sussex and co-editor with Eileen Yeo of *Popular Culture and Class Conflict 1590–1914* (Brighton, 1984).

11. WHAT IS
DIPLOMATIC HISTORY . . . ?

*The record of what one clerk said to another clerk? The
history of what men think they are doing? The tittle-tattle
of Embassy underlings? The history of relations between
states? The story of the decisions that make war and peace?
What is diplomatic history?*

D. C. Watt

The practice of international history, that is of the history of relations
between nation states, began in the nineteenth century with the
publication, first, of the great series on international treaties, and
then of national diplomatic documents pioneered by the British
official blue books and followed by the national publication of
documents on the origins of the Franco-Prussian war and on the war
of 1914–18. Most historians of nineteenth-century Europe were,
even in the early 1950s, essentially historians of European diplomacy, rather than, as today, historians of the domestic developments of one or two European countries. The first Chairs of
international history in Britain were founded at the London School
of Economics and Chatham House in reaction against the development of nationalist historiography. Their holders, Sir Charles
Webster and Professor Arnold Toynbee were prohibited, in the
cause of world peace, from teaching history from a national
viewpoint, a prohibition as resolutely ignored by the former as it
was practised (save in the case of the Palestinians) by the latter.

Webster was primarily a historian of British foreign policy. Since
his retirement in 1952, however, the subject he taught has developed greatly, alongside more traditional studies of British foreign
policy, from the history of European diplomacy in the national sense
to that of international relations in the much larger sense, compre-
hending not merely diplomatic relations outside Europe but also the
strategic, economic and sociological aspects of international developments. More recently the great outburst of theoretical work on
international relations in the United States between the mid-1950s
and the mid-1960s has been adapted to the study of international
relations in general, and of international crises in the Far East by (in
particular) Christopher Thorne at Sussex University. In Leeds,
studies in the use of, and institutionalisation of propaganda in the

broadest sense have been developed. In London emphasis has been placed on the machinery of international negotiation as well as on economic and strategic factors. Work is now in progress on the role of trades unions in diplomacy, on international financial diplomacy and, alongside Professor Milward's new pioneering work on the development of European integration after 1947, on the growth of permanent political institutions in Western Europe and in the Atlantic region.

In Europe, parallel developments in France around Professor Duroselle and his followers and in Italy in the long tradition of the 'history of Treaties and International Relations' begun in the pre-Fascist era have recently joined with the British strain in the foundation of a separate International Commission for the History of International Relations, which made its debut at the 1985 World Historical Congress at Stuttgart.

It is curious however that, to judge from recent public discussions of the development of the study of history in Britain, these enormous developments, in which British historians are in the forefront, have passed virtually unrecognised in Britain, even by their fellow academic historians. Endless debate on high versus low history, social history, women's history, ecclesiastical, urban, economic, intellectual history fragment the profession as much as they entertain it. The model held out is that of the *Annalistes,* whose whole thrust is to reduce the role of the individual human to invisibility and to seek identifiable patterns in the manipulation of – often suspect – statistics.

The study of international history lies at the opposite pole to such developments. Concerned as it is with the history of 'high politics', its *dramatis personæ* are insufficiently numerous and anonymous to escape identification. Concerned, like microphysics with the study of individual behaviour patterns over what are, relative to the concerns of the *Annalistes,* micro-seconds of time, the student of international history finds himself confronting the accidental, the misunderstood, the misapprehended and the misconceived. The source materials are as full and rich as the personnel are few. The international catastrophes in the study of which international history originated are so universal in their impact that accusations of trivialisation demean only those who make them. The research has the fascination of detective work, some requiring the meticulous timetabling of a story by Russell Thorndyke, others the leg work of the 87th Precinct, others the psychological insights of a Simenon, a Van der Velde or a Le Carré. The writer of detective fiction however deals with an artificially closed world of his own invention. The international historian lives in the middle of the consequences of the events, the actions, the decisions and the indecisions he studies.

Whatever the original impulse towards the study of international history, the historian who comes to his subject of study to condemn, cannot but stay to stare, to contemplate and to understand. Since the subject of study is the behaviour of individuals in society his work is entwined with and draws upon that of those social scientists who are similarly engaged. It was not only the contempt of the *Annalistes* for students of *l'histoire événementielle* which led, for example, to the development of international history in France being more connected with the *École des Sciences Politiques* than with the Sorbonne.

There is a nemesis however in store for the historian of international relations in the future. It lies in the multiplication of national governments in the world and of agencies of national governments concerned with international relations. Twenty British departments of government now maintain permanent missions abroad. Multiply that by the number of nation members of NATO and OECD and one can project a lifetime of research devoted to the study of Anglo-American relations under Margaret Thatcher and Ronald Reagan. In thirty years time this will no longer concern me: today's students may be forgiven if they turn to such absorbing (but less exhausting) subjects as the history of the garden in seventeenth-century England or thaumaturgy in medieval Cornwall.

Simon Adams

Like all subdivisions of historical study, diplomatic history is an artificial construction. At the most basic level, it can be described as the analysis of relations between states, employing what are known as diplomatic archives: treaties, reports of ambassadors, accounts of negotiations, policy memoranda and so forth. Since the emergence of permanent agencies of diplomacy in the sixteenth century, these archives have been among the best preserved (and easiest to read) in western Europe. They have long been an established source for historical research. To the extent that the study of diplomatic negotiations 'might be of great use to those gentlemen that shall be bred up to serve princes in this kind of honourable employment' (as the editor of one of the earliest collections of diplomatic documents to be printed in England, *The Compleat Ambassador* of 1655, put it), the subject needed no further justification. In the nineteenth century, when *der Primat der Aussenpolitik* and the central role of international relations in both history and contemporary politics were generally accepted, such scholarship was also of self-evident importance.

The growth of social and economic history in the present century, which has both inspired and reflected the widely-held view that social and economic forces lie at the root of historical causation, has relegated diplomatic history to the position of a narrow and old-fashioned specialisation. Like all such specialisations, it becomes an immediate target of parody; subjects like the consular service in Luxembourg in the eighteenth century or the fate of the Sanjak of Novi Bazar are immediately conjured up. Nor have diplomatic historians helped their case by retaining a Foreign Office view of the world, in which the conduct of diplomacy is the concern of a small body of ministers and ambassadors. Such a rarified approach has not only crippled the subject, but it is also misguided. The relationship between domestic and foreign policy is always a symbiotic one and should be studied as a whole. It is no accident that the most exciting works on diplomatic history to appear in recent years, those of Fritz Fischer and his students, for example, or Paul Kennedy's *The Realities behind Diplomacy*, have dealt specifically with the non-diplomatic forces involved in the making of foreign policy. For all its reliance on hostile gossip, Seymour Hersh's study of Henry Kissinger in *The Price of Power* provides a far more revealing picture of the political realities of American diplomacy in the Nixon years than do the Doctor's own memoirs.

Such involvement of wider forces and interests in the formulation of foreign policy is not a creation of the twentieth century. Even in the most absolutist monarchies of the sixteenth and seventeenth centuries, it could never be fully isolated from other concerns. War and diplomacy were not simply the sport of princes. Even the most apparently personal aspect of royal diplomacy – dynasticism – reflected the wider attitudes of contemporary society. Kings who pursued obscure dynastic claims at the cost of war shared the same mental world as subjects who would spend years and fortunes in litigation over disputed inheritances. Commercial lobbies, the providers of loans, made sure their interests did not suffer. Moreover the Reformation created a wider public throughout Europe, with strong views on how international relations ought to be conducted. Even if these views can be dismissed as expressions of religious bigotry, they nevertheless represented the articulation of a significant body of public opinion. The concern of all contemporary governments with propaganda is in itself a revealing comment on how seriously this public opinion was taken. Henry IV of France, it should be remembered, was assassinated by one of his subjects who opposed his foreign policy on religious grounds. The reaction to the proposed Spanish Marriage in England in the 1620s is a significant example of the limitations on the ability of monarchs to conduct their diplomacy freely. Charles II's credibility never really recovered from the exposure of the secret treaty of Dover.

Diplomatic history is not, therefore, the simple chronicling of negotiations, but an attempt to provide a balanced appreciation of the complex forces that shaped foreign policies. Kings, ministers and governments took certain steps at certain times for certain reasons. Occasionally their decisions were frivolous, occasionally 'ad hoc responses to a constantly changing situation' occasionally carefully planned, and frequently the product of long and bitter debate. Elizabeth I and her council argued over intervention in the Netherlands for fifteen years between 1570 and 1585. To describe these debates and the negotiations that resulted from them as fruitless is to miss the point. Why Elizabeth did not intervene prior to 1585 is as important a question as why she did then. Studies of her foreign policy (as with any other) demand not simply an account of the international situation, but also a recreation of the mental world of Elizabethan politics, in which the Netherlands debate was as much a catalyst as a product. To a greater degree, perhaps, than most other fields of historical research, diplomatic history is concerned less with what men do than with what they think they are doing.

Roger Bullen

The short answer to the question is that it no longer exists; diplomatic history has for decades been incorporated into the wider framework of international history. Its critics might say it has merely changed its name but this is not the case. How and for what reasons, has diplomatic history become international history?

Diplomatic history emerged in the nineteenth century as the study of statecraft, the conduct of foreign policy at the highest level in the state, what G. P. Gooch called 'Courts and Cabinets'. It was a dominant strand in the new 'scientific history'. Historians thought that by gaining access to the archives of states they could reveal the secrets which explained their rise and fall. Their histories were revelations both in the sensational and in the biblical meaning of the word; they revealed the secret stratagems of monarchs and statesmen and they revealed the pattern of the past which explained the present. The great strength of nineteenth-century diplomatic historians was their determination to record a formal narrative of what actually happened. Their principal weakness was their nationalist bias; in their histories nations and states were cast as heroes and villains. Indeed their histories came to mirror the conflicts of their age. The triumph of nationalism in nineteenth-century Europe confirmed the dominance of diplomatic history in historical studies; it alone was capable of providing the 'key' to the present. The history of nations became the story of diplomacy and war. This was what was taught as history in schools and universities. In the age of imperialism Europe's past acquired a universal significance. When Evelyn Waugh visited the Belgian Congo in the 1920s he found the nuns at a Mission School teaching the native children the history of the Italian Wars of the sixteenth century. This kind of history was never without its critics both for what it said and what it left out. Engels in his book *The Role of Force in History*, published in 1877, which was a study of the founding of Bismarck's Germany, majestically swept it aside.

In the half century before the outbreak of the First World War, significantly new perspectives were added to the study of the relations between states. They came from the critics of the European social, political and economic order. Diplomatic history was largely isolated from these developments: it remained on the *piano nobile* of the recent past where kings led their armies into battle and peace was upheld by family alliances. Liberals and Socialists argued for a different version of events. They examined the social and economic origins of imperialism and the way it transformed the European state system into a global international order. They observed the rules by which this state system operated and assessed the likelihood of their breakdown. They questioned, and some rejected, the notion of a 'just war'. They campaigned to subject 'secret diplomacy' to public scrutiny and they introduced the concept of an arms race. They discerned the importance of a complex international economy and charted the effects of trade and tariff barriers on the relations between states. All these ideas and perspectives became a framework for a new international history, the study of the relations between states and societies in all their aspects. The outbreak of war in 1914 provided a new generation of historians, many of them profoundly disillusioned during the war with the doctrine of nationalism, with the opportunity to use the new tools of analysis. Confronted with the chaos of total war historians felt the need to look for new explanations of what had happened. It was natural that they should turn to the ideas of the men who had warned of the dangers.

In the inter-war years in Western Europe and in North America the best traditions of diplomatic history were incorporated into international history. It was the liberal historians who were responsible for this fusion. They stressed the importance of a formal narrative, of a need for a chronological understanding of what had happened before August 1914. They rejected the notion of a capitalist and imperialist order inevitably doomed to self destruction. They looked for 'guilty men', particular individuals who had taken decisions which led to war. As a consequence international history became a broad and humane branch of historical studies. The search for deep rooted explanations for the behaviour of states and the examination of the structure of international society was tempered by a proper regard for the actions and responsibilities of individuals.

In the fifty years after the Treaty of Versailles international history flourished. The questions it posed about the origins of wars were of fundamental importance both to the recent history and, it seemed, to the future of mankind. Governments began to publish their diplomatic documents on a massive scale both to justify their actions and to explain to ordinary men and women why it was that their families and their homes had been devastated by war. These documents, dismissed as dull by those who have not read them, in fact deal with every aspect of the relations between states. In the late 1960s and 1970s a reaction set in and, in western Europe at least, international history came under attack. New branches of historical enquiry asserted themselves by denigrating the traditions and achievements of well established rivals. Others disliked international history because of its preoccupation with the exercise of power. It was also in the 1960s and 1970s that historians in western Europe realised that the fate of mankind had passed out of the hands of those who ruled them. It seemed to some that the importance of Europe's recent past had diminished. When France ceased to be a great power with imperial interest across the world, French historians virtually ceased to write international history. By contrast in the United States involvement in the Vietnam war fuelled a bitter controversy among historians about America's role in world affairs since 1945.

It is my conviction that the recent unpopularity of international history is a temporary phenomenon. The retreat from narrative which was so characteristic of the 'new' history of the 1960s and 1970s has been reversed. Social historians for example have 'rediscovered' narrative and now write histories of individual peasants and prostitutes. In this new age of narrative revival it is merely a matter of taste to prefer one type of narrative to another. On this argument alone there is ground for new optimism among international historians. There is further hope for renewed interest as the moving frontier of the archives takes us into the period after the Second World War. It is not difficult to predict that controversies about the origins, nature and course of the Cold War will replace those about the First and Second World Wars. Indeed they already have among American historians. In western Europe we shall soon catch up.

Although it is true that some historians think they are divided by the subjects they study, it seems to me they are united by the fact they all have a story to tell and in the telling we all pose some wrong questions and give some wrong answers. History is what historians write; the past is something different.

Kinley Brauer

Students of American diplomatic history have traditionally been at a disadvantage. Specialists in European diplomatic history have dealt with a system in which intergovernmental relations were a primary concern and foreign policy was created and implemented by extraordinary personalities. European diplomats were often élite, cosmopolitan, and highly trained. Throughout American history, international relations have nearly always played a role secondary to domestic issues, and the most interesting problems have often centred around partisan politics and competing regional, ethnic, economic, social and (to a lesser degree) ideological conflicts. Furthermore, since the United States has generally lacked a professional diplomatic service and has most often chosen its diplomats according to a political spoils system, American secretaries of state and diplomats have, with a few outstanding exceptions, not been especially interesting as subjects of study.

Since the Second World War, however, the study of American diplomatic history and diplomatic history generally has broadened to encompass far more than simply intergovernmental exchanges. With the development of Marxist analysis in its varied forms in Europe and its maturation after 1945 and the development of revisionist literature on international relations in the United States in the 1950s, diplomatic historians have shifted emphasis from political relations among nations to economic relations, ideological and cultural patterns, and the domestic sources of foreign policies.

Initially, American scholars tended to become less interested in how policies were implemented than in how they were created; more interested in purposes rather than effects; and more concerned with broad, enduring trends rather than discrete crises. Focus shifted away from foreign offices to much wider and all-encompassing bases. One of the consequences of this shift in approach in the United States has been the gradual disappearance of the phrase 'diplomatic history'. During the 1950s and 1960s, diplomatic history was replaced by 'foreign policy'.

By 1970, the pendulum swung back from an emphasis on domestic sources of foreign policy towards a consideration of actual diplomacy, and a synthesis of the two thrusts emerged. 'Foreign relations' has become the dominant definition in the speciality, signified by the creation in 1967 of the Society for Historians of

American Foreign Relations and the recent publication of the important bibliographic *Guide to American Foreign Relations Since 1770*.

This new approach may be seen in recent examinations of American imperialism, which became a topic of renewed interest among non-Marxist, revisionist American historians in the early 1950s. Drawing upon the insights of British historians John Gallagher and Ronald Robinson, American scholars first began exploring the American commitment to economic imperialism in terms of the establishment of an 'open door' around the world for American goods. By the end of the next decade, scholars had examined the role of special economic interests, political theorists, and military strategists in creating a 'new American empire'.

In the 1970s, diplomatic historians began looking at the means by which the United States carried out this imperial thrust in formal diplomatic relations with the great powers and developing nations. Others explored non-economic sources of imperial thought in the United States and aspects of cultural imperialism overseas, which often required an intensive examination of the politics, economics, and society of other nations as well. Diplomatic historians today thus consider virtually every aspect of American society and culture and those of a great many other nations as well.

As a field of inquiry, diplomatic history provides the basis for a richly complex study of domestic development, comparative history, and international harmony and conflict. It requires a serious examination not only of one actor in an international setting, but of many actors, and when well done enriches one's understanding of the historical nature of all, thus serving as a prism for the examination of many other fields of history.

Akira Iriye

Diplomatic history is one of the oldest fields of history; the term 'Rankean' in the sense of modern historical scholarship originally referred to the historian's stress on exhaustive research in the diplomatic archives. Since then, diplomatic history has been approached in many ways, but it has retained one characteristic that distinguishes it from other fields: it encompasses more than one country's history, for there can be no diplomatic history where there are no foreign affairs, and no foreign affairs unless there is more than one country involved.

Diplomatic history, then, is a study of the history of relations among nations. Broadly put, diplomatic historians' methodologies and approaches may be divided into four categories. The first is the most traditional approach, the multi-archival method. It entails the examination of available documents to reconstruct past dealings of governments with one another as reflected in the evidence. This approach calls for linguistic abilities and patience on the part of the historian, as well as an eagerness to show many sides of an issue. Well-balanced chronicles of diplomatic negotiations result from such research.

The second approach is more endogeneously oriented; while studying diplomatic questions the historian will be primarily interested in the domestic sources of a country's foreign policy. The decision-making approach which has been utilised by political scientists as well as historians fits into this category. They will examine the pressures – social, economic, political – that are brought to bear on policy makers as they define their government's position on a diplomatic question. Foreign affairs, in this approach, are virtually indistinguishable from domestic affairs; diplomatic history becomes what German historians call *gesellschaftliche Geschichte*. Marxist studies of foreign policy also fall into this category.

The third category may be termed the systemic approach. Diplomacy is analysed in terms of changing patterns of overall international relations, what some call 'world systems'. The international system as a whole is examined, whether in terms of patterns of alliances, global strategies, imperialism, colonialism, or economic linkages. The whole globe is seen as a system, and various regions of the world as sub-systems, each developing its own rules of the game, and constraining the freedom of choice on the part of nations ('actors'). An example would be 'the Washington Conference system', a system of treaties and understandings that developed in Asia during the 1920s. It defined the frameworks in which various countries acted and it was sustained by a regime of economic interdependence.

The fourth approach is what may be called cultural or intellectual. International relations are seen as intercultural relations. Historians who pursue this line of inquiry assume that policy makers as well as citizens are products of culture; their memories, emotions, prejudices, ideas – their 'mentalities' as some call them – must be taken into consideration in studying foreign affairs. The subject becomes more complicated as diplomatic historians have to deal with more than one people. They have to be comparativists in that sense; they are required to know something about the cultures of the countries whose relations they discuss. But an analysis at this level can yield insights into images and perceptions that peoples have of themselves and of each other. Moreover, it helps broaden diplomatic history to include such topics as educational exchanges, missionary activities, tourism, and the transfer of technology. It also enables the historian to explore the possibility that different peoples may share much despite their historical differences. For instance, I have tried to show that by studying the Second World War as a cultural as well as a power-level phenomenon, one gains an understanding of how much enemies had in common in terms of their ideologies, images of war, and visions of peace.

Thus diplomatic history, at its best, is synonymous with human history. It is a field that can and should be enriched through the collaboration of historians in all countries. If only for this reason, it ought more properly to be called international history.

FURTHER READING

Bass, H. J. (ed.), *The State of American History* (see particularly Evans, L., 'The Dangers of Diplomatic History' and McCormick, T. J., 'The State of American Diplomatic History') (Chicago, 1970); Billias, G. A. and Grob, G. N. (eds), *American History: Retrospect and Prospect* (see particularly May, E. R., 'The Decline of Diplomatic History') (New York, 1971); Cowling, M., *The Impact of Hitler* (Cambridge, 1975); Dezell, C. F. (ed.), *The Future as History* (see particularly Leopold, R. L., 'The History of United States Foreign Policy: Past, Present and Future') (Nashville, 1977); Haines, G. K. and Walker, J. S. (eds), *American Foreign Relations: A Historical Review* (Westport, Conn., 1981); Hunt, M. *et al*, 'Symposium: Responses to Charles S. Maier, 'Marking Time: The Historiography of International Relations', *Diplomatic History*, 5 (1981); Iriye, Akira, 'Culture and Power: International Relations as Intercultural Relations', *Diplomatic History*, 3 (1979); Joll, J., *The Origins of the First World War* (London, 1984); Kennedy, P., *The Rise of Anglo-German Antagonism, 1860–1914* (London, 1980); Kennedy, P., *The Realities behind Diplomacy* (Glasgow, 1981); Lyons, F. S., *Internationalism in Europe, 1815–1914*, (Leyden, 1963); Meier, C. S., 'Marking Time: The Historiography of International Relations' in Kammen, M. (ed.), *The Past Before Us: Contemporary Historical Writing in the United States* (1980); Ramsay, G. D., *The City of London and International Politics at the Accession of Elizabeth Tudor* (Manchester, 1975); Renouvin, P. and Duroselle, J. B., *Introduction to the History of International Relations* (trans. Ilford, M.) (London, 1967); Sutherland, N., *The Massacre of St. Bartholomew and the European Conflict, 1559–1572* (London, 1973); Taylor, A. J. P., *Struggle for Mastery in Europe* (Oxford, 1954); Toscano, M., *Storia del Trattati e Politica Internazionali* (two vols) (Turin, 1965); Watt, D. C., *Succeeding John Bull: America in Britain's Place, 1900–1975* (Cambridge, 1984); What *about the People? International History and the Social Sciences* (London, 1985); Wernham, R. B., *After the Armada* (Oxford, 1984); Wohl, R., *The Generation of 1914* (London, 1980).

THE CONTRIBUTORS

Simon Adams is Lecturer in History at the University of Strathclyde and is completing a book on *English Foreign Policy, 1529–1640*.

Kinley Brauer is Professor of History and International Relations at the University of Minnesota. He is the author of the 'The Diplomacy of Expansionism, 1821–1861' in William H. Becker and S. F. Wells, Jnr, *Economics and World Power: An Assessment of American Diplomacy Since 1789* (Columbia, 1984).

Roger Bullen is Senior Lecturer in International History at the London School of Economics and editor of *The Political Correspondence of Lord Palmerston and Lord Clarendon, 1833–7* (HMSO, 1985).

Akira Iriye is Professor of American Diplomatic History and International History at the University of Chicago and author of *Power and Culture: The Japanese-American War, 1941–1945* (Cambridge, Mass., 1981).

D. C. Watt is Professor of International History, University of London, and author of *Succeeding John Bull: America in Britain's Place, 1900–1975* (Cambridge, 1984).

12. WHAT IS
EUROPEAN HISTORY . . . ?

*The totality of national histories? The history of the rise of
the western world? Shorthand for the central zone of the
capitalist world economy? Continental history with Britain
left out? With Russia left out? What is European history?*

A. J. P. Taylor

**European history is whatever the historian wants it to be. It is a
summary of the events and ideas political, religious, military,
pacific, serious, romantic, prosaic, near at hand, far away, tragic,
comic, significant, meaningless, anything else you would like it to
be. There is only one limiting factor. It must take place in or derive
from the area we call Europe. But as I am not sure what exactly that
area is meant to be, I am pretty well in a haze about the rest.**

Paul Dukes

Hundreds of millions of us call ourselves Europeans, but do we
know what our history is? All of us go to school, and learn at least a
little of our past there, but even for those who become professional
historians, the focus is more national than continental. Yet European history must be more than the sum total of its constituent
parts.

There are many difficulties in the way of discovering what this is.
The meaning of the very word 'Europe' is not clear, its origins lost in
the mists of East Mediterranean antiquity. Its roots have been traced
by various experts to suggest a range of meanings: 'broad eye' or
'broad face'; 'dark (derived from 'dank decay') face'; 'evening' or
'west' (from the setting of the sun). Dank decay and the setting of
the sun certainly seem appropriate to some commentators, who
look upon an effete Europe sinking with the rest of Atlantic
civilisation as the world's centre moves over to the dynamic basin of
the Pacific.

Another problem about Europe is its boundaries, metaphorical
and real. Classical writers looked upon it primarily as the northern
littoral of the Mediterranean, thus creating a line of thought that led
down to the opening statement of H. A. L. Fisher's famous

textbook: 'We Europeans are the children of Hellas.' Those historians who work on (and/or amid the remnants of) more northerly civilisations would want to insist that we are also the children of Celtic, Germanic, Norse and Slavonic parents, to name but four. And then, where are the actual boundaries of the continent set? At Cabo da Roca, there's no problem. If you go any further, you fall down a cliff. At the other end, however, travellers on the trans-Siberian railway have to be reminded that they are leaving Europe by a signpost stuck in gently rolling hills appended to the Ural Mountains.

Whether or not to place Russia in Europe has long been a vexed quesion. So has another, should Britain be in or out? For some insular historians, the continent is still cut off. When we cross the Channel, we encounter at least one major state – Germany – that has often been considered to be a different kind of exception in Europe. Moreover, the concept of an Atlantic civilisation growing up since the Second World War has included Britain and the USA along with a Europe from which Germany has often been excluded and Russia, in both pre- and post-revolutionary guises, nearly always kept out.

Confronted with exceptions of various kinds, we have to ask, where is the rule? Is it France? French historians might welcome this award, although a certain duality is to be marked in their attitude, which contains a simultaneous insistence on the uniqueness and universality of their national experience. In this respect, they carry a trait that can be found in Britain and the USA to an extreme degree, perhaps under what they perceive to be a threat from the Anglo-Saxons or English-speaking union. Certainly, German historiography since 1945 does constitute an exception in the sense that there has been little or none of this duality. But the Russians would conform here, since the Soviet Union's forceful re-entry into Europe has been accompanied by a vigorous assertion of the more general applicability of the pre-war experience of socialism in one country.

The Western rule consists of what is considered to be the 'normal' transition to modernity. This involves a revolution, especially France in 1789 but also the USA in 1776 and Britain in 1649 or 1688. In each case, absolutism was overthrown, and the way thereby prepared for the establishment of a variety of representative government. Against this, at least some historians of Germany would argue that the transition to modernity can be made without a revolution or even without representative government, while developments in Britain, the USA and France alike were themselves not really 'normal'. Apologists for the USSR would want to add that the Revolution of 1917 constituted the transition of human development to a new level beyond modernity.

Now that they have lost their world dominance to the USSR and the USA, the states in between might produce a greater number of historians capable of throwing off the blinkers of nationalism and the restrictions of the exception-rule model to answer more completely not only the question, what is European history, but also other questions equally important: what is its relationship to the history of the peripheral super-powers, and to that of the wider world? As they produce answers to these questions, the historians will perhaps help the citizens of Europe to make educated choices of any alternatives which may still come their way.

Immanuel Wallerstein

European history, it seems to me, can have three quite different meanings.

Europe can be defined geographically, using current continental boundaries. We can assume that each contemporary state in Europe has a 'history', and that 'European history' is the summation of these state (or national) histories.

This approach poses a few technical problems: are the USSR and Turkey, to be considered in or out of this 'Europe'? Where do we include the story of pan-European structures (which in no case includes all of the states)? But these are minor problems, and such a history of Europe can be written with little difficulty. Indeed, it often has been written. Many of our textbooks present precisely such a history.

The roots of this approach can be found in the combination of the widespread nineteenth-century assumption about the social primordiality of the states with the Ranke-ian injunction to write history *wie es eigentlich gewesen ist*. If states were the true matrix of social life, and history was their history projected backward in time, then Europe's 'meaning' was in the totality of the history of these states.

Europe can be defined culturally, as a particular civilisational tradition, that of the 'West', that of (Judeo-)Christianity.

In this case, European history is the history of the 'rise' and perhaps of the 'decline' of the 'Western world'. There are technical problems here too. Are its 'roots' to be found only in ancient 'Greece', or with both the Greeks and the Hebrews? In the present, are Europe's 'extensions' – the United States, Australia, etc. – part of 'Europe'? Is the 'east' of Europe – Byzantium, Orthodox Christianity – part of this Europe or a second, separate 'civilisation' sharing some millenial past but long since separated from Europe? What should be done about an anomalous zone like Albania? But once again, these are minor problems. Answers can be offered for all these queries, and indeed have been. European histories of this kind can and have been written, and were particularly popular in the quarter-century following the Second World War.

The roots of this approach can be found in the 'expansion of Europe', which reached its geographical apex in the last third of the nineteenth century and its cultural apex in precisely the quarter-century following the Second World War. If Europe (then the United States) 'dominated' the world, there must be some explanation of this remarkable phenomenon. It was comforting to locate it in a millenial cultural quest of Western man for human freedom.

Europe can be defined as a convenient shorthand for the central zone of the capitalist world-economy, as it has developed historically since the long sixteenth century.

In this case, European history (which then ought properly to be qualified as 'modern' European history) is the story of the genesis and functioning of a particular historical system which originated in Europe (although it has since spread to cover the world) and within which segments of geographical Europe have played a central role from the beginning until now. This approach also poses technical problems. It is clear that the 'central zone' of the world-economy included the United States by the late nineteenth century, and Japan today. On the other hand, many parts of geographical Europe were in the beginning peripheral or semi-peripheral zones of the world-economy, and some still are today. But once again these technical problems are not insuperable, once one has a clear grasp of the economic processes of this historical system.

The roots of this approach are to be found in material and political reality, and are indeed institutionalised in such contemporary structures as the OECD. No doubt it becomes dubious to designate this central zone as 'Europe' other than as a convenience. There is however one justification for doing this. The myth of Europe, as reflected in the second approach, can be thought to be an outcome of precisely the economic structure which the third approach des-cribes. In the classic words of W. I. Thomas, 'if men define a situation as real, it is real in its consequences'. If the core of the world-economy has been termed in shorthand as Europe, then this concept of Europe has had very real consequences, and is thereby a worthy subject of historical analysis.

These three competing visions of Europe, and hence of European history, will continue to vie with each other. New ones may arise. Our choice can only be in function of the questions we wish to resolve, the choices we wish to make. Such a choice has no objective basis outside real history. The choice of our historiography is itself part of the historical process.

Douglas Johnson

Historians study the problems of human beings living in societies. Therefore the matter of history is not fixed according to geographical divisions, or according to the disposition of continents. In any case, Europe is neither a fixed quantity nor a determinate area. General de Gaulle's appraisal of a Europe which exists from the Atlantic to the Urals is both inadequate because it does not allow for what lay and lies beyond, and it is inadequate because it encompasses such a wide diversity. Nevertheless, there is a subject which should be called European history.

European history is not a sequence of events, as occurs in national histories. European history consists of a series of crucial epochs. It begins with that of late antiquity, when Greek and Roman worlds, linked to the Orient, Asia Minor and the Mediterranean, disappeared. Then, in the eleventh century, there was the Investiture conquest and the assertion of a Christian society. Later we see the sequence of what is (to Europeans) a familiar process. Renaissance and Reformation, the exploration and the conquest of the world, the formation and consolidation of nation states, capitalism, industrialisation and colonialisation. There is a story of science, of humanism, liberalism, socialism. There are dramatic revolutions in the interior of certain European states; there are wars between these same states (stretching particularly from the Thirty Year's War to the Second World War). These crucial epochs were experienced by all European countries. It was at different times, in different ways, with particular resonances. But they form a shared experience. They therefore form a framework for historical study which is not only valid, it is also inescapable.

Of course, Europe is not a continent, it is a prolongation of Asia. Europe has always been affected by the world beyond: Gibraltar, Constantinople, the Urals, are not outposts behind which Europe can furtively shelter, they are the routes through which Europe has been penetrated. If an historian, over-influenced perhaps by the study of French history, asks if Europe is a person, then he will receive no satisfactory account of who that person is. Europe has never physically or politically been one (except, arguably, for brief moments during the Roman Empire and the reign of Charlemagne).

However, should one ask what Europeans have done, in a relatively short period of history, then it is easy to establish a similarity between the inhabitants of the towns and villages of Europe, which constrasts with those peoples whose origins were outside Europe. The European coloniser was unlike those who were colonised, the European scientists did not resemble scientists elsewhere. European industrialist were, for many years, unique. In the study of European history, there are periods when the dominant role is played by certain countries, by Portugal, Spain and the Low Countries, for example. Then they disappear from the forefront of the historian's preoccupations (thus proving that the historian is an historian of Europe), to be replaced by Britain, the empire formed around Austria, and Germany. The boast of the French is that France always forms a major element. Hence the mistake of many historians who have always believed that European history is French history.

Europe is not a nation. It has been compared to an orchestra. There are moments when certain of the instruments play a minor role, or even fall silent altogether. But the ensemble exists. In European history, the element of timing, or of time, is all important.

There is also the element of judgement. In national histories it is possible to talk about the decline of Spain, to claim that at a certain point French history took a wrong turning, to pinpoint the malaise of German society, to ask what went wrong with the *Risorgimento*. But in European history such judgements do not occur. European history consists of many unresolved contradictions. The analogy of music is appropriate, since music, like theatre and like the novel, is the expression of a European identity which has spread throughout the world. Sometimes this has been seen as an achievement. (Borges once said that Argentinians and North Americans are Europeans in exile.) Sometimes as an oppression (Aime Cesaire, the black Caribbean poet, wrote that he carried on his back not only the road and the taxes of the Commandant, but also the God of the Commandant).

Guizot, lecturing at the Sorbonne in the 1820s, believed that the distinctive characteristic of European history was diversity. Other societies, he claimed, had unity and simplicity, and it was the very existence of such diversity and conflict which made for the progress and vigour of Europe. Perhaps it was natural that a Frenchman should have such beliefs because it is also claimed that the very diversity of France is the essence of French civilisation. But it is significant that it is a Czech, Milan Kundera, someone from a state that was manufactured in 1919, who has expressed his regrets that Europeans have so easily accepted the division of Europe into east and west which is the result of the Second World War. He expresses a nostalgia for a Europe that is all embracing. In 1458 Pius II, in his *Treatise on the State of Europe* began by describing Hungary, Transylvania and Thrace. This is a certain idea of Europe, one of communication, exchange, receptivity. Its history is there to be explored.

Marc Raeff

When I was a schoolboy in France in the 1930s, the answer to the question 'What is European history?' seemed simple and obvious: since France is in Europe, any place, event or personality that has a relationship to France belongs to European history (nay, to history *tout court*). But since I have become an historian of Russia, the question elicits a more complex and ambiguous response.

An historian of Russia looks at 'Europe' so to speak from the outside, from its periphery. The Russians themselves, at any rate in modern times, have tended to speak in terms of 'Europe' and/or 'Russia' (often without further defining either the terms or the relationship between them). This was not always so, of course. I do not believe that Kievan or Muscovite sources down to the end of the sixteenth century refer to Europe. They knew of Byzantium and they were quite aware of the differences in creed that separated them from 'heretical' neighbours to the West as well as from 'pagans' to the East. Since religion largely determined self-image and identity, some sense of belonging to a Christian continent must have existed; yet the divergences mattered more than the similarities, so that Muscovites felt different from their Catholic (or Protestant) neighbours to the West.

As contacts with states West of the Polish-Lithuanian Commonwealth became more intense and continuous in the sixteenth century, 'Europe' became a source of a few special and rather exotic contributions to the tsar's environment (Kremlin palaces and churches, decorative silver plate, fanciful techniques such as printing). All this did not suggest anything very problematical in the nature of 'Europe' and of its relationship to the tsar's realm.

The situation changed in the second half of the seventeenth century, for Muscovy established lively trade, diplomatic and cultural contacts not only with neighbouring Poland, but with German states, Sweden, England, Holland and Italy as well. It is interesting to note that the contemporaries of Peter the Great (1689– 1725) referred to 'Europes', in the plural, demonstrating their awareness of both the unity and diversity of the world that lay West of Poland and Mount Athos. After the reign of Peter the Great, as far as the élites were concerned, there was no longer any question as to Russia belonging to Europe, though the specific nature of this belonging remained ambiguous and an open question. The ambiguity remained – even waxed greater – as 'Europe' (not more precisely defined) was set up as a model, or measuring stick, for Russia's perception of its own social, economic and political development. In other words, the Russian élites sought to define

Russia's identity and self-image in 'European' terms. Quite clearly, therefore, European history had to provide the categories and concepts that helped the Russians to understand Russia and its situation in the world.

Yet the feeling that late seventeenth and early eighteenth century Russians had had of the existence of several Europes should be taken seriously. It was possible, indeed necessary, to be selective in one's borrowings from 'Europe'; and this realisation readily led to a hierarchy of 'Europeanness'. Thus Poland, Russia's immediate neighbour, was hardly seen as 'Europe'. Similarly, the Balkans (in the widest cultural sense); and the Mediterranean world were relegated to the 'exotic' fringe of Europe, to be neither imitated nor emulated.

In the final analysis, Europe *sunsu stricto* came to mean the German core of Central Europe, France and England (and for a short time Holland too). Thus it was the Europe of the 'well ordered police state', of the Enlightenment, of industry, of bourgeois and constitutional governments that provided the yardstick and categories of self-identification. In the twentieth century, the United States was also seen as a mere extension of Europe, a more developed and effective instance of the 'European' (now western and modern) model and criterion.

Since this Europe was the standard by which the Russians gauged and defined themselves (it mattered not whether they did so approvingly or critically), the Russian historian has to study and understand the European conditions of relevance to Russia at a given time and with respect to a given issue. In so doing he or she realises that not everything of prime importance to Russia has necessarily been of prime importance to Europe. He is also more alert to the consequences that European models or precedents may have in another environment. He is thus more sensitive to the contradictions between intentions and practice, to the impact of the imminent manifestations of a trend, to shifting interactions when a given European element is transferred to another society. To give an example from my recent research experience: to understand and explain the nature of legislation and the intellectual development of Russia in the second half of the eighteenth century I was led to a study of European models which inspired them. This brought me to the realisation that the models were not those of contemporary France or England (that is the Enlightenment of Voltaire or Rousseau, Physiocracy, *Standestaat* monarchism as in Prussia) but rather the culture of the early *Auflarung* and the practices of the *Policeystaat* and Cameralism of late seventeenth-century Central Europe. Furthermore, it became quite clear – at least to me – why these influences had quite different results in Russia: the institutional and social means available to Russia's ruler and élites forced adaptations that in the long run had effects which were almost the opposite to those in the societies from whence the influences had originated. I would submit that something of the same sort is occurring today in the case of the influences exercised by the Soviet Union (and its 'Europe') on the so-called Third World.

As a discipline, history is in truth a 'European' creation, and preeminently a modern one (with its roots, of course, in classical Greece and Rome). Its concepts, problems and intellectual presuppositions are basically all 'European'. Not surprisingly, therefore, the efforts of Russian intellectuals to break loose from this European framework and to mark off Russia clearly from 'Europe' have been conditioned by the very same European intellectual trends from which they wish to cut loose (e.g. Slavophilism in the nineteenth century, Eurasianism and 'neo-Slavophilism' in the twentieth). This should call our attention to the historical and 'European' foundations of our conceptual framework and vocabulary, and to this end we have to understand the phenomena and trends in European societies that gave rise to them. Is this not best done from the perspective of the 'outsider', as well as the insight of the participant?

Like the Muscovite contemporaries of Peter the Great and Louis XIV we should distinguish between several 'Europes' – both geographically and chronologically. There is no single European history, but rather many – each relevant to a specific problem and context.

Eva Haraszti

The term European history means in Britain, Continental history. For Continental historians European history includes the history of Great Britain as well.

I do not think the term European history can be an exact one. One can speak about European culture; and geographically Europe is a continent, but one can only speak about the history of France, of Germany, of the Soviet Union, that is about a history of an individual country. If one speaks about a region of Europe, again one could call eastern, southern, northern histories, European histories.

There were many centuries when history meant European history. When other continents were not discovered or there were no literate people in those continents who could have narrated their stories.

I have mainly carried out research on nineteenth and twentieth-century history: looking at Palmerston and the Hungarian Revolution of 1848–49, at Kossuth in England in mid-Victorian times, at Appeasement, at Hitler's invasion of the Rhineland, at the Anglo-German agreement of 1935, at Chartism and at Britain and Hungary between 1945–55.

If we accept the view that British history belongs to European history, the themes above are all European themes. But if we look closer, we would find that none of them were exclusively European subjects.

Consider Chartism for instance. Everyone knows that the post-Chartist period is connected with Australian and American history, where many Chartists emigrated or were deported.

Or consider Kossuth in mid-Victorian England. He first entered Britain in the autumn of 1851, later he went to America and came back in 1852 to live half a decade in Britain. However nearly all his speeches and activities relate to his experiences in America.

The Rhineland question in the mid-1930s, the Anglo-German Naval Agreement and Appeasement are all themes in British-German or British-German-French relations. Whenever and wherever Britain is included in a theme, it becomes extra-European history because the consideration of British politics and diplomacy in these periods were always imperial. Even when Britain lost or gave up her Empire, the considerations of her politicians either on the right or the left remained Empire-centred – perhaps with the honourable exception of the efforts of Attlee. But then as an excellent recent study (R. Smith and J. Zametica, 'The Cold Warrior', *Journal of International Affairs*, Spring, 1985) has demonstrated, he did not entirely succeed.

At the Institute for Historical Research of the Hungarian Academy of Sciences in Budapest, we used to have a department which was called World History, or the Universal History Department. And the Hungarian Historical Association carried out a national census to find out which universities and teachers were researching into world history. Both the Association and the Institute hold the view that without knowing, understanding and investigating world history, Hungarian history cannot be properly understood or evaluated. Hungarian history is the story of emigration; sectors and leaders fled abroad for political, religious or economic reasons from the beginning of the eighteenth century. The Hungarian diaspora, representing nearly half of the population of the mother country is now spread across the world. Yet their history belongs to a small Eastern European country as well as to world history.

Economic historians of the last centuries hardly use the definition of European economic history. The economic history of Europe is understood more and more to be a vital part of world economic history.

FURTHER READING

Auty, R. and Obolensky, D. (eds), *Companion to Russian Studies. Vol. 1: An Introduction to Russian History* (Cambridge, 1976); Barraclough, G., *History in a Changing World* (Oxford, 1955); *An Introduction to Contemporary History* (Harmondsworth, 1967); Barker, E., Clark, G. and Vaucher, P., *The European Inheritance* (three vols, Oxford, 1954); Berl, E., *L'Histoire de l'Europe* (three vols, Paris, 1946, revised 1973); Dehio, L., *The Precarious Balance: The Politics of Power in Europe, 1494–1945* (London, 1963); Halecki, O., *The Limits and Divisions of European History* (London, 1950); Harding, S. and Philipps, D., (with Fogarty, M.), *Contrasting Values in Western Europe* (London, 1986); Hay, D., *Europe: the Emergence of an Idea* (Edinburgh, 1957); Krejci, J. and Vitezslov, V., *Ethnic and Political Nations in Europe* (London, 1981); Lichtheim, G., *Europe in the Twentieth Century* (London, 1972); Mazour, A. G., *Modern Russian Historiography* (Princeton, 1958); Raeff, M., *Understanding Imperial Russia* (trans. Goldhammer, A.) (New York, 1984); Szamuely, T., *The Russian Tradition* (edited with an introduction by Conquest, R.) (London, 1974); Vernadsky, G., *Russian Historiography: A History* (ed. Pushkarev, S., trans. Lupinin, N.) (Belmont, Mass., 1978); Wittram, R., *Russia and Europe* (London, 1973).

THE CONTRIBUTORS

Paul Dukes is Reader in History at the University of Aberdeen and author of *A History of Europe 1648–1948* (London, 1985).

Eva Haraszti is author of *The Invaders: Hitler Occupies the Rhineland* (London, 1983).

Douglas Johnson is Professor of French History at University College, London, and the editor of the Fontana *History of France*.

Marc Raeff is Professor of Russian and Modern European History at Columbia University and author of *Understanding Imperial Russia* (New York, 1984).

A. J. P. Taylor is the author of many books including *Struggle for the Mastery in Europe 1848–1918* (Oxford, 1954) and *The Origins of the Second World War* (London, 1963). His most recent book is *How Wars End* (London, 1985).

Immanuel Wallerstein is Distinguished Professor of Sociology at the Fernand Braudel Center, New York, and author of *The Politics of the World Economy* (Cambridge, 1984).

13. WHAT IS
THIRD WORLD
HISTORY . . . ?

Disposing of the problem of non-European history? A
commodious brantub? Dustbin history? A progressive
variant of colonial history? An invitation to bland
generalisation and a blindness to complexity? A fertile
ground for modernisation theorists? A study in richness and
diversity? What is third world History?

M. E. Yapp

'The Soviet Union', *The Times* informs us, 'is a third world economy
with first world weapons.' That statement may indicate what a
slippery concept is 'the third world'. The term has been used in
three ways: as a residual category after the abstraction of the Old
World and the New; as another residual category after the abstraction of the Communist East and the Capitalist West; and as a
shorthand for describing those parts of the world with the lowest
standard of living. Depending upon which definition is chosen
different countries will comprise the third world and, although the
categories overlap, decisions about inclusion and exclusion will
always be arbitrary. The historian of the third world needs an axe
before a pen.

The present fashion, as indicated by *The Times*, is to use the term
to denote poor countries. On this basis the central question of third
world history must be why these countries became or remained
poor and that is a dismal starting point for the study of the richness
and diversity which has marked the development of the cultures of
the countries concerned. To aspire to write an extended historical
introduction to the Brandt Report is a miserable ambition for any
historian. Further, third world history in this sense can relate only to
the last two hundred years at most, since the present discrepancies
of wealth did not exist in earlier periods; accordingly, much of what
makes the history of these countries of interest will be omitted.
Another consequence must be the divorce of individual countries
from their cultural background; China, Afghanistan and Paraguay
certainly qualify as third world countries but their regional neighbours Japan, Saudi Arabia and Uruguay do not.

The vogue for third world history springs from four main impulses. First is a superficial notion of relevance, which at the global level holds that the great problem of the future will be the relationship between rich and poor countries. Adherents to this view improbably contend that the problem may be more easily resolved by a study of history, and at the domestic level assume, against all the evidence, that greater understanding leads to greater tolerance and therefore wish to teach non-European history in British schools.

Second is a curious sentimentality which, confusing the study of history with the study of the past and disregarding the nature of history, believes that the poor must have a history as well as the rich.

Third is a zeal for cheap display. The core of history teaching in British schools and universities is British and European history and, outside a few specialised centres, there is little money available to provide either the books or teachers to cover the rest of the world. Determined to provide some exotic and deceptive icing to the cake, historians search for a convenient container for the rest of the history of mankind. In earlier times this receptacle was imperial history, which fell into disfavour as being Eurocentric and regarding the rest of the world as a plastic mass moulded by Europeans. Now, shorn of some of its former burdens, imperial history survives as a serious and coherent intellectual discipline but its place in the curriculum has been taken by third world history which has many of the disadvantages of imperial history without the compensating unity provided by the thread of empire. As presently practised, third world history is a commodious brantub in which scholars and students rummage bravely and hopelessly, pulling out their treasures of *bric à brac and* exposing them in a vast historical jumble sale.

The fourth attraction of third world history is that it is easy; with so much of the world to cover there is no point in studying it in any language but English.

Third world history is merely the latest, condescending device for disposing of the perennial problem of describing the history of the non-European world. Like the division of the history of the world into a small number of regions defined by strategy and sentiment, it is an evasion; for no system of categories can succeed if it does not make it practicable for the historian to come to grips with his basic source material through command of the necessary languages and by sitting down with his raw material. Writing the history of the non-European world is as serious an undertaking as the study of the history of Europe; it is no different in kind although the difficulty of the source materials may make it a more laborious venture. There is no substitute, therefore, for studies of countries, of regions of countries and of cultures, or for training historians in the basic skills of their disciplines and the languages of their sources. Realistically, therefore, the serious study of the countries of the non-European world is likely to be carried on in the countries themselves and in a few specialised centres outside which can afford the library collections and the specialisms which are required. If a fraction of the resources consumed by historians tinkering with the history of the modern Middle East was devoted to the proper exploitation of the Aladdin's cave of the Ottoman archives, the subject would be transformed.

Other historians may feed profitably off the work of the specialists. For them the challenge is to find some way of integrating the history of the countries of the non-European world with the history with which they are familiar. Hiding non-European history in a dustbin labelled 'third world' is not an answer.

C. A. Bayly

To many Asian, African and Latin American historians, and to the educated populations for whom they write, the term 'third world history' is not only meaningless but insolent. For them it seems the most recent attempt by Europeans to define them not in terms of their own identities, histories and traditions but in terms of what they are not: in this instance, 'white', 'advanced' or 'affluent'. The term 'third world' with its overtones of poverty and backwardness also arouses the cultural and, less worthily, racialist attitudes of the élites of these new nations. Latin Americans do not like to be lumped in with Indians, whatever the rhetoric of non-alignment or anti-imperialism. Indians do not see themselves in the same category as Africans.

People outside Europe understand their development in the context of quite different histories. To Muslims – from West Africa to Indonesia – the proper context for their history is the history of Islam as a world religion. In many Pakistani schools, for instance, history ends with the death of the last great Muslim emperor, Aurangzeb, in 1707 and begins again with the Pan-Islamic movement in defence of the Turkish Khalifa of 1918–22. Even for Indians and for Chinese who have been deeply affected by the secular categories of Marxist thought, the *longue durée* of history is determined by Institutions and cultures of India and China and the impact of the West is seen as a disruptive but temporary phase.

Asian, African and Latin American critics of the notion of 'third world history' are right to see it as little more than a modern, progressive variant of colonial or 'native' history. In the eighteenth century Europeans began to put the history of the rest of the world into a comparative framework. But the yardstick was always European politics and culture. The notion of 'oriental despotism' was a reflection of the attack on absolute monarchy in Europe. The attempts to find a chronology for Indian history were related to the scientific dating of the Bible; Sanskrit attained its prominence in the academies of Europe less because of an interest in Indian history than because it was seen as forefather of Latin and Greek. In the nineteenth century colonial history was written around the triumph of European society over native misrule. Indians and Africans were rarely more than a backdrop to the doings of colonisers, missionaries and merchants. Independence struggles and the rise of liberal academia converted imperial history into 'Commonwealth and Overseas History' or the history of the 'Expansion of Europe'. But the view remained – and remains – resolutely Europe-centred. 'third world history' seems to be the old colonial history, but with colonial administrators reduced in stature and an emphasis on the 'impact of the world economy'.

Yet, like Rousseau's God, Europe may need the label of 'third world history' even if it does not represent a coherent field of study. The concept is a compromise between those European and English historians who remain wedded to the idea that the rest of the world is peripheral and historians of Asia, Africa and Latin America who are determined to smuggle their specialities into the educational system under any rubric, however limiting. Of course, there *are* common features in the history of Africa, Latin America and Asia so that historiographies can be compared and methodologies transferred from one area to another. To a greater or lesser extent all these continents were affected by formal or informal colonial rule. All were drawn into a system of world trade dominated by the west; in all these continents, again, people who worked on the land were affected by movements in world prices and sometimes reacted in similar ways.

But comparison is not the same as amalgamation. Ultimately it must be the histories of particular societies which gave depth and intellectual justification to the academic study of history. 'third world history' does not really exist, but we must pretend that it does in order to prevent the histories of 80 per cent of the world's population being pushed to the margins of historical education.

Gervase Clarence-Smith

The least productive way to define third world history is to begin by setting geographical limits. Many people are surprised to learn that Japan is not just included in the course I teach on the third world since 1800, but actually plays a central role in the course. The reasons for investigating the history of an 'over-developed' nation such as Japan lie in a definition of third world history based on process rather than boundaries. Historians of the twenty-first century, if they ever exist, will probably see the two greater problems of our own century as the threat of nuclear holocaust and the cleavage between a rich 'north' and a poor 'south'. It is this latter issue which lies at the heart of third world history. How did this 'global rift', as Leften Stavrianos has called it, come into existence, and what are its dynamics? Before the industrial revolution, poverty was the lot of most people everywhere in the world, and the consciousness that one part of the world is far more affected by poverty than the rest is a relatively new one. This in turn gives third world history two of its most distinctive characteristics, a strongly economic bias and a clear concentration on the period subsequent to the industrial revolution. In some ways, third world history can thus be seen as a branch of modern economic history. And yet, the controversies which rage over the origins of a world divided along fault lines of poverty bring into play more than the factors discussed in traditional and narrow forms of economic history.

The fundamental divide between historians is crisply and clearly set out in Frances Moulder's provocative, if ultimately unsatisfactory comparative study of China and Japan in the nineteenth century. On the one hand, there are those who blame the Western states for using their new-found industrial strength to prevent the rest of the world from developing. The historians in this camp broadly adhere to ideas of 'underdevelopment', and are widely credited with a left political perspective. However, such explanations of the roots of third world poverty are also exploited by reactionary nationalists and even Fascists. At the same time, some Marxists, most notably Bill Warren, have strongly rejected the hypotheses of underdevelopment theory, and have stressed the progressive nature of imperialism, in terms of the development of the forces of production. Marxists of this opinion note the fact that Marx himself considered that British colonialism in India was progressive from this point of view.

On the other hand, there are those who stress internal obstacles to economic development within the poor countries of the world. Although often considered right-wing and reactionary, this school of thought ranges all over the political spectrum. Genetic and racist theories have been discredited since the fall of Nazism, at least in scholarly discourse, but the debate over the contribution of ecology, culture and social structure is still very much alive. Perhaps the most interesting strand in this debate is the one using 'modes of production' analysis, inasmuch as it attempts to combine all these elements in order to understand the roots of poverty.

Perhaps, it is now clearer why Japan plays such an important part in this story. It is the best example of a country which *did* develop although it was both submitted to the pressures of imperialism, through the unequal treaties, and characterised by distinctly non-Western forms of culture and society. Moulder, who espouses an underdevelopment perspective, tries to explain away the phenomenon by arguing that Japan was less subjected to imperialist pressures than any other third world region, through a fortunate combination of distance and sheer luck, but her argument is simply not supported by the evidence. I find much more convincing those arguments which stress the peculiarities of Japanese society and economy, such as high rice yields, precocious urbanisation, proto-industrialisation, a well-developed bourgeois class buying its way into the *samurai* gentry, high levels of literacy, and great national cohesion around the powerful symbol of an emperor who reigned rather than ruled. More recently, the 'hyper-growth' of South Korea and Taiwan, in spite of their great degree of subjection to the United States, has again tended to favour arguments stressing endogenous social phenomena.

Another debate which strengthens the view that the key to the poverty of nations lies in internal factors is the contrast between the fate of Argentina and that of New Zealand and Australia, examined by Donald Denoon. All three countries in the nineteenth century concentrated on the export of bulky agricultural produce, often exactly the same commodities, and were heavily dependent on Britain. But Argentina had a land system which favoured huge *latifundia* over medium-sized farms, a ruling class ideology with strong relics of feudal and *rentier* elements, substantial illiteracy, and a proletariat dominated by anarchist rather than trade unionist values. This debate again underlies the need to look at the countries which succeeded as well as those which failed to develop. After all, the *reductio ad absurdum* of the underdevelopment perspective is that no country apart from Britain should ever have industrialised.

Christopher Abel

For Europeans Latin American history is usually perceived as a 'new' subject. This is not true of Latin American historians, who have penned substantial volumes about their own continent for a century and a half. National schools of historiography began to take shape from the 1830s, when the evolving national élites, like those in post-independence Africa and Asia, began to rewrite history both to justify their own ascendancy and as an instrument for instilling patriotism amongst literate minorities. Liberal writing stressed that independence marked a creative rupture with an obscurantist past dominated by an inquisitorial Church and an exploitative metropolis. By contrast, Conservative interpretations emphasised the creative vitality and pioneering spirit infusing the Iberian colony. Out of these debates came significant historical works, the most important of which was probably Lucas Alamán's five-volume history of Mexico. Even Ecuador could boast a three-volume history published in the 1890s by the Archbishop of Quito, Federico González Suárez, who was denounced as a cloistered cuckoo by his ultramontanist colleagues, refugees from the Carlist Wars in Spain and the *Kulturkampf* in Germany, for whom a war to extinction against Liberals was a higher priority than historical scholarship.

A tradition of bureaucratic order inherited from the Iberian colony and reinforced by positivist influences imported from Latin Europe in the late nineteenth century was manifest in the foundation of national libraries, archives and historical journals and in the publication in the early twentieth century of skilfully arranged volumes of historical documents. To these were added at the centenary of the independence wars numerous biographies of national heroes and their precursors.

Since 1945 these traditions have interacted with other trends: empirical historical investigation along the lines of the English-speaking countries; the pursuit of theoretical models and their practical application by Marxist-Leninists; the search for the historical roots of economic underdevelopment and social inequalities by the first generations of professionally-trained neo-Keynesian economists and social scientists; and case-studies by social anthropologists and sociologists at the level of the village, the enterprise and the urban residential district. While a new interest in the quantifiable was nurtured by new technocracies trained in statistics, new archives were thrown open by, for example, the agencies expropriating large estates during the Peruvian agrarian reform of the 1960s.

Pragmatic moves towards closer connections between Latin America and Africa and Asia have been evident since 1945 in bids to influence the Non-Aligned Movement, co-operation between oil producers, and armament sales and military engagements. These political trends have made similar impact upon the historiography, apart perhaps from the Cuban revolutionary drive to rehabilitate the African past. There is a space in the Latin American historiography for more studies of family history, popular religion and oral culture, that use the techniques so fruitfully employed in sub-Saharan Africa.

But is this to ask for a third world history? Or to plead for more comparative study and further methodology cross-fertilisation? Perhaps the notion of a third world history has outlived its usefulness, constituting no more than an invitation to bland generalisation and a blindness to complexity that was common among modernisation theorists, who, in the 1950s and early 1960s, treated Latin America, Asia and Africa as a *tabula rasa* for mechanistic theorising undersubstantiated by evidence. This is not to query the significance of the history of the three continents. Just as in the eighteenth-century assumptions about the nature of man that European intellectuals cherished were challenged by exposure to non-European societies, so too in the late twentieth century the South poses inescapable challenges to Northern assumptions about the international distribution of power and wealth. Discussion of what constitutes a 'state of nature' has been supplanted by debate about what constitutes a 'natural economy'. While the North-South debate continues and the future of underdeveloped countries remains the most pressing problem facing the world, the continued vitality of the study of their history can be assured. For the next half-century it can be confidently forecast that the history of Latin America, Africa, and Asia will require no apology.

Gordon Johnson

It is difficult to define 'third world history' because it is impossible to determine exactly what is meant by (as Geoffrey Elton puts it) 'that curious extra-terrestrial place known as the third world'. Even if you accept some workaday definition of the 'third world' as consisting of most of the economically poorer countries of Africa, Asia and Latin America, there is no sense in which they can have a coherent history: where is the unity of place or of people, the shared language, religion or culture, the similar economic or social development, let alone a common political tradition? They simply do not exist; to manufacture connections between these countries results in a superficiality and a depreciation of the historical experience of most of the human race. Nor can we say that the separate and independent histories, each worth doing in its own right, of India or China, Mexico or Malawi, Belize or Brunei, go to make up 'third world history', in the way that the history of Cheshire is part of England, or the story of France part of Europe.

The term 'third world' implies connections with other worlds. It was coined to describe those parts of the world which had once been colonies of the western powers, and it became common currency after the collapse of the colonial empires in the mid-twentieth century when imperialism went out of favour. 'Third world history' might profitably have been seen, then, as describing the relationship between the West (another ambiguous term) and its former colonies. This relationship, or rather, complex relationships, include more generally those between rich countries and poor ones, between developed economies and under-developed ones, and between powerful states and weak ones. Moreover, in much of what is written there is the suggestion that the poverty and weakness of the 'third world' remain intimately bound up with the way in which they were and are linked to the more dynamic economies and dominant politics of the West. In a sense, therefore, 'third world history' is but good old-fashioned imperial history writ large.

What of course, casts doubt on the utility of even this rough working definition is that over the past forty years the study of imperialism has advanced so far, and so too has our understanding of the internal dynamics of colonial societies. We are now much more aware of the subtle interdependences which exist between societies and economies. Once, imperial history was regarded as a branch of constitutional history or a sub-division of European foreign policy, and the dominant role of the imperial powers in world affairs was taken for granted. Now we are no longer so sure. It is a perverted historiography that sees Africa, into which Europe could fit over a dozen times, as having no history before the advent of the Europeans, or whose modern history is a consequence solely of European interference, just as it is a travesty to consider the history of China over the past two centuries as a response to the opium trade. Even in the case of India, historians have become increasingly aware of the resilience of its society and of the limited capacity of imperial rule to change its forms and its economy; while Latin America, which received much European settlement, money and trade, seems perversely to have continued on its own way. Moreover, relationships between countries tend to shift in time and are always two-way: yesterday's thriving trade and investment are gone today; a close political tie of old becomes of no consequence in a new power-play. Britain's nineteenth-century economic development may have been intimately connected with her capacity to draw upon foreign resources: but that was a dependent relationship from the perspective of the metropolis also, and it carried with it implications for domestic as well as overseas developments.

'Third world history', then, can embrace complex issues of the connections between peoples, economies and states, and in particular the continuing relationships stemming from old imperialisms. But as the unifying generalities implied by 'third world history' give way to concrete historical examples, the thing itself disappears beneath our gaze.

Christopher Fyfe

Anyone who teaches African history has to contend with Hegel's dismissive words, 'At this point we leave Africa, not to mention it again. For it is no historical part of the world'. It is true, not many people have read Hegel's *Lectures on World History*. But his dismissal lingers on: year after year my students tell me how incredulous their friends are when they tell them they are studying African history.

What Hegel was saying is that only Europe counts, that history only makes sense in a European perspective. How his message was interpreted in colonial days was that only the white man counts, that history only makes sense seen through white eyes. This is how history was presented during the years of colonial rule. When colonial rule ended it was time for a new viewpoint. Historians could then remove their blinkers and try to see the view from Africa, instead of the white man's view of Africa, they began to notice that Africa is indeed an historical part of the world. In Africa, over the millennia, people have lived satisfying lives, have devised their own distinctive political systems and religions, their own technologies and their own beautiful artefacts. Historians could also notice that the white man's history had ultimately led to the subjugation of millions to alien rule and economic exploitation, to mass slaughter on an unparalleled scale, to nuclear warfare and the extermination camps of Hitler's Europe.

A new dimension was thus added to world history. It no longer needed to be written as the history of Europe and its extensions. Over the past decades the proliferating scholarly historical work on Africa, drawing on the allied disciplines of archaeology, social anthropology, botany and linguistics, has refocused and greatly enriched the study of history.

Hence, though the details of African history may not be of any particular relevance to British students, one can justify teaching it to them as an exercise in salutary self-criticism. Its message is that however much Africa may have been subjected to foreign rule or pressures, Africans were not just mindless pawns who only entered history when they began to be exploited and conquered by Europeans, but that, like the other peoples of the world, they have their own historic identities as active participants, not merely as passive victims.

It was, I suppose, too good to last. Now, in our present Reagan–Thatcher era, the inevitable retaliatory backlash strikes back, as 'Third World History'. Here is a label that can safely restore to the whites their direction of the historical process. Historians who use it are going back onto a well-trodden path. Polarising the world into two categories again (the 'Second World' has somehow dropped out – rather like the old Second Class on the pre-war railways) brings us back to the familiar division of colonial days, we/they, whites/ natives, history/no history.

Those lumped together as the 'Third World' have only one thing in common – their being victims of the other 'world'. In no other way could one meaningfully bracket together the histories of, say, Nigeria, Indonesia, Fiji and Peru. Nothing else unites them historically. To treat them simply as components of a notional 'Third World' is to restore them to the purely passive role they were assigned in colonial days. The ascription 'Third World' is meaningless unless it is set against a contrasting 'First World'.

For however this amorphous category is defined, its implicit meaning is clear. Those who fall into it are no longer active but passive, and can therefore be dismissed with Hegelian condescension. It is not even for them to determine whether or not they are members of it, any more than it was in the past. Under racial rule – in the old British Empire, in Nazi Germany and still today in South Africa – it has always been for the dominant race to decide who belonged in which racial category. Occasional Indian princes, or 'honorary Aryan' Jews, or (in South Africa) the wealthy Japanese, might be admitted to the club. So with the 'Third World'. China, it seems, is privileged to remain outside. India is inside. And what of Brazil, or Mexico, or Saudi Arabia? In or out? It is not for them to choose. The decision rests with the self-appointed determinants of the historical process, the new Hegelian hegemony.

So, as part of the 'Third World', Africa (except perhaps white South Africa) will once again be 'no historical part of the world'. It will only rate attention in so far as it exemplifies to what extent the 'First World' has, or has not, exploited and oppressed it. Its history has to start with its common relationship to the other victim members – that is, with the moment of foreign impact – just as it did in the old historiography. 'What is Third World history?' I am asked. I can only answer – the imperfectly disguised backlash of the old Eurocentric historiography.

FURTHER READING

Albert, B., *South America and the World Economy for Independence to 1930* (London, 1983); Barthold, V. V., *La Découverte de l'Asie* (Paris, 1947); Barrington Moore Jnr, *Social Origins of Dictatorship and Democracy* (Harmondsworth, 1967); Bethell, L. M., *Cambridge*

History of Latin America (Cambridge, 1985 -); Brown, J. M., *Modern India: the Origins of an Asian Democracy* (New Delhi and Oxford, 1985); Denoon, D., *Settler Capitalism: the Dynamics of Dependent, Development in the Southern Hemisphere,* (Oxford, 1983); Fieldhouse, D. K., *Colonialism, 1870–1945. An Introduction* (London, 1981); Franginals, M. M. (ed.), *Africa in Latin America* (New York, 1984); Geertz, C., *The Interpretation of Cultures* (New York, 1973); Holland, R., *European Decolonisation 1918–81* (London, 1985); Hopkins, A. G., *The Economic History of West Africa* (Harlow, 1973); Kedourie, E., *The Chatham House Version and Other Middle Eastern Studies* (London, 1984); Latham, A. J. H., *The International Economy and the Underdeveloped World,* (Beckenham, 1978); Leventhal, A. (ed.), *Armies and Politics in Latin America* (New York, 1978); Long, N., *Towards a Sociology of Rural Development* (London, 1977); Marshall, P. J. and Williams, G., *The Great Map of Mankind* (London, 1982); Moulder, F., *Japan, China and the Modern World Economy* (Cambridge, 1977); Pollard, S., *The Idea of Progress* (Harmondsworth, 1971); Porter, B., *The Lion's Share: a Short History of British Imperialism* (Harlow, 1984); Robinson, R. and Gallagher, J. (with Alice Denny), *Africa and the Victorians* (London, new ed. 1981); Said, E., *Orientalism* (London, 1978); Stavrianos, L., *Global Rift: The Third World Comes of Age* (New York, 1981); Seal, A., *The Emergence of Indian Nationalism* (Cambridge, 1968); Steadman, J. M., *The Myth of Asia* (London, 1969); Wakeman, F., *Conflict and Control in late Imperial China* (California, 1976); Warren, B., *Imperialism, Pioneer of Capitalism* (London, 1980).

THE CONTRIBUTORS

Christopher Abel is Lecturer in Latin American History at University College, London, and co-author with Colin M. Lewis of *Latin America: Economic Imperialism and the State* (London, 1984).

C. A. Bayly is Smuts Reader in Commonwealth Studies in the University of Cambridge, and author of *Rulers, Townsmen and Bazaars. North Indian Society in the Age of British Expansion, 1780– 1870* (Cambridge, 1983).

Christopher Fyfe is reader in African History at the University of Edinburgh, and author of *Africanus Horton: West African Scientist and Patriot* (Oxford, 1972).

Gordon Johnson is Lecturer in the History of South Asia at Selwyn

College, Cambridge, and author of *Provincial Politics and Indian Nationalism* (Cambridge, 1973).

Gervase Clarence-Smith is Lecturer in the History of Africa at the School of Oriental and African Studies, University of London, and author of *The Third Portuguese Empire, 1825–1975* (Manchester, 1985).

M. E. Yapp is Professor of the History of the Near and Middle East at the School of Oriental and African Studies, University of London, and author of *Strategies of British India* (Oxford, 1980).